MONA AND URIAH'S GUIDE TO PLANNING A DESTINATION WEDDING

by
MONA GABALLA
AND
URIAH HAKALA

authorHOUSE™

1663 LIBERTY DRIVE, SUITE 200
BLOOMINGTON, INDIANA 47403
(800) 839-8640
WWW.AUTHORHOUSE.COM

First published by AuthorHouse 01/17/06

ISBN: 1-4208-4090-8 (sc)

Printed in the United States of America
Bloomington, Indiana

This book is printed on acid-free paper.

Contents

1 Introduction **1**

2 Foreword **5**

3 Overview/Section Arrangement **6**

4 Where do I start? The Basics **7**

    4.1 The Growth of Destination Weddings 7

    4.2 Is a Destination Wedding Right For Me? 8

    4.3 Common Misconceptions 12

    4.4 Budget... 14

    4.5 What Kind of a Wedding Do You Envision?........ 20

    4.6 Picking a Date 23

    4.7 Choosing a Destination.................................... 24

        4.7.1 What to take think about when deciding where to go? 24

        4.7.2 Narrowing Down Your Results.................. 30

        4.7.3 Making a Final Selection.......................... 32

5 Planning Trip...**34**

6 Picking a Hotel/Ceremony/Reception Location 44

7 Where to marry? Ceremony ideas and types ... 46

8 Reception Details **47**

        8.0.1 Wedding Packages 49

    8.1 All Inclusives 51

    8.2 Non-All Inclusives 52

    8.3 Boutique Hotels... 52

8.4   Alternate Ceremony/Reception Locations.......... 52

    8.4.1 Villas 52

    8.4.2 Restaurants 53

    8.4.3 Bed & Breakfasts 54

    8.4.4 Cruises 54

    8.4.5 Wedding Chapels – Vegas Style............... 55

9   Should I work with a Wedding Coordinator? .. 56

10 Should I work with a wedding coordinator? Questions to ask... 59

    10   Selecting Vendors and Vendor Relations 61

    10.1 Selecting a Photographer............................... 62

    10.2 Selecting a videographer 63

    10.3 Entertainment... 64

11 Attire 65

12 Guest Lists – How to invite and Who to invite? 67

13 Save the Date 69

14 Planning a weekend/Hosting Multiple events 71

    14.1 Multiple Events – Things to Think About.......... 72

    14.2 Rehearsal Dinner... 73

15 Planning Guest Travel................................. 75

    15.1 Working with a travel agent 76

    15.2 Airfare... 77

    15.3 Hotel Bookings 78

    15.4 Transportation 80

16 Wedding Party..**81**

17 Planning the Honeymoon **83**

18 Etiquette...**84**

    18.1 Who pays for what? 84

    18.2 Tipping..85

    18.3 Gift Registry & Shower 87

    18.4 Inviting Guests to other activities 87

    18.5 Out of town gift bags 88

19 Nice extras **90**

20 Planning tools/tips **92**

    20.1 Workbooks 92

    20.2 General Information – Where to start? 93

21 The week of the wedding **95**

22 Last but not least – 14 Extra Hints **96**

23 Planning an At Home Reception....................**99**

24 Destinations and cruise info – Popular ones and ways to obtain info..**101**

    24.1 US Destinations..101

    24.2 Cruise Weddings: 102

    24.3 Foreign Destinations: 102

25 Conclusion **106**

26 Appendix 1 – Additional Templates and Resources...**107**

    26.1 Wedding Timeline 108

    26.2 Itinerary Template 115

26.3 Sample RSVP Response Wording....................117

26.4 Sample Wedding Budget...............................117

26.5 Electronic Wedding Planner...........................120

26.6 'Day of' Template 121

26.7 Planning Trip Information Template 122

26.9 Planning Trip Summary Template..................124

26.10 Day of Itinerary for Wedding Party 125

26.11...126

26.12...127

27 Appendix 2 – Legal Requirements for various locations 128

1 Introduction

My fiancé and I got engaged, and, both being consultants and liking to travel, we wanted to find something out of the ordinary and off the beaten path for our wedding. It was a no-brainer decision to look into having a "destination wedding". Although a lot of our research showed that destination weddings were on the rise, and even though the Today show was in the process of planning a destination wedding, we had a hard time finding any comprehensive written literature about this chic, fun, new "trend".

So, where to start? Every wedding magazine and book seemed to be filled with loads of useful information, unfortunately, there was nothing specific to destination weddings in anything we were able to find. After many unsuccessful trips to Borders, Barnes n Noble, and the Walgreens on the corner for ridiculously expensive wedding magazines, we were at a loss. So we just decided to research the idea of having a wedding in the city where we lived, Chicago.

Our main goal? We decided if we were going to be having a wedding in town, we wanted to do something somewhat unique and different. We had loads of friends and family that did the typical church wedding with a banquet hall reception. While these ceremonies were beautiful, elegant, and lovely, they just weren't our cup of tea. We both like to do things a little off the beaten path, and a little different. With our main "goal" in mind, we went to work – researching various outdoor venues, historical societies, museums, restaurants, etc. Based on some of the initial quotes we received from caterers and various restaurants, in order to plan any sort of unique event, we would be spending much more than our budget would allow. Yes, we both make decent salaries, but we are also both reasonable - $60,000 for a big party was just a little much for us...could we do it? Yes. Did we want to? No.

We were stuck – we were unable to put together the kind of celebration that we wanted to in our hometown, and our first, original idea that sounded so ideal to us – small group of friends and family, barefoot on the sand at sunset, was so overwhelming to plan – we just didn't know where to start.

Luckily, with a little persistence, a few different resources, lots of caffeine, and countless hours spent surfing the web, we were able to begin planning the beachfront "destination" wedding of our dreams.

Overwhelmed? You're certainly not alone, so were we! We had hundreds of questions – what country to marry in, what location to marry in, what type of wedding to have, where to stay, legal requirements for

marriages in different countries, the list was endless....
Although the information is out there, I was unable to find anything that thoroughly consolidated all of the issues, problems, and questions that we had into one resource. With this book, I hope to put my own research and time spent to work for you so that you can organize yourself a bit better than we were able to when we first started planning. Does this book have all the answers for every issue you will run into? No. Will it be able to structure your thoughts and planning process into main areas so that you are better able to plan? Most definitely!

Planning any type of wedding can be a little stressful, to say the least, but planning a wedding in a remote location can be even more so. Hopefully these tips, thoughts, and info will help to make things easier for you. It would, of course, be impossible to put all of the information specific to many various locations into one publication, what this initial book should serve to do is provide a guide to you – help you set some parameters around the things to think about when you begin planning a destination wedding, and some creative approaches to getting answers. I wish we had had a resource like this available to us when we began planning!

Regardless of where you plan to marry and how you plan to marry, always remember – you have your fiancé, someone that you will be spending the rest of your life with. It's easy to get caught up in all of the other wedding drama, but, if you keep coming back and reminding yourself of that important point, it will help to add some sanity to the wedding planning. Always remember that the most important part of your wedding day is what is right for the two of you. While it is nice to be sensitive to other personalities and opinions, you'll drive yourself crazy focusing on others. Always be true to yourselves and what suits the two of you, after all, as much as the wedding industry has been hyped up, at the end of the day, your wedding day is really about nothing other than the two of you! Good luck, happy reading, and congratulations!

2 Foreword

While I offer my opinions and comments freely in this book, it is merely a frame of reference for you. Everyone is different, and what may be a great idea for one person or couple is just not suited for another. Try to take my suggestions and put them to work for what is right for you.

3 Overview/Section Arrangement

In each section, I want to provide three things: First, I'd like to give an overview of the topic at hand. Second, I want to provide our solution to the problem, just for your information so that you can get a feeling for what we went through. Finally, I will offer a section of questions or tips for you to keep in mind while going through your own decision making process.

Knowing the right list of questions to ask yourselves is the number one thing to remember when creating a successful destination wedding and avoiding problems and stress. Regardless of whether you are making decisions between the two of you, talking to your vendors while planning, or government agencies when considering legalities, being well prepared and confident in what you need will save many headaches and make sure you get exactly what you are looking for.

4 Where do I start? The Basics

4.1 The Growth of Destination Weddings

Destination weddings are on the rise:

Ten percent of the 2 million American couples that marry each year now say their vows away from home in what are called "destination weddings," a **200** percent increase in the last decade, according to Conde Nast's Bridal Group Infobank and Modern Bride magazine.

For its part, **Beaches Negril** hosted 606 nuptials in 2003. The **Sandals and Beaches Resorts** chain held **11,527** weddings at its 18 properties in Jamaica, Antigua, Bahamas, St. Lucia and Turks and Caicos in 2003.

This market is obviously very much on the rise. Couples looking for wedding destinations would be happy to have some options outside of the Beaches and Sandals of the world that currently are the most well known that cater to wedding parties. We ran into problems finding a lot of information outside of these chains. Hopefully the information in subsequent chapters will help you with some of the questions we had initially as to how to go about planning.

4.2 Is a Destination Wedding Right For Me?

Our guess is, if you have this book in hand, you're probably thinking about going the destination-wedding route. I urge you to make sure that this is the right choice for you. It takes a lot of planning and coordination to put together a wedding in a remote location, and, while worth it, it will be easier to go back on your decision when you run into a roadblock unless you have thoroughly thought through the pros and cons and have decided that a destination wedding is the way you want to go.

We ran into many different issues throughout the course of our planning, and almost changed our decision to have a destination wedding multiple times. We ran into problems with resorts over quoting us, questions about the pricing of travel, and even wondering whether or not we would be able to capture the feel of what we were looking to attain within our budget. We also had pushback or general disapproval of our far away plans from friends and family that would be unable to make it. Because we did not know what were in for when we originally started, we were easily frustrated and almost went back on our decision. I am not trying to scare you – I just want you to know the problems that we ran into so that you know the things you should take into account before you go full steam ahead.

What exactly is a destination wedding anyway? A destination wedding can involve just the two of you, or a group of friends and family along with the two of you, or any number of guests that you would normally invite to a wedding. The reception is more like a big party and can be held at the destination with an optional additional celebration when the couple returns home (an at home reception – which will be discussed more later).

A destination wedding can be fairly seamless to plan for a few different reasons – many resorts and cruise lines have made it very easy to wed on-site due to full time staffed wedding coordinators with a knowledge of various country's legal requirements for marriage. Many also offer convenient and reasonably priced wedding packages to cover ceremony basics (photography, judge, cake, toasts, etc.) There will be further discussion of wedding packages in a later chapter.

You will want to begin planning as soon as possible, not only to reserve your venue, but also because fulfilling marriage requirements of the country you will be getting married in may take some time. Some countries may require document translation, residency requirements, etc. so get on the ball – and, if you are as anal as I am, you will need as much time as possible to ensure that all of your details are addressed and all of your questions are answered. Additionally, you may need more time because extra elements are involved.... You will need to plan travel for nearly everyone, and since you are going to a location away from home, you may need to do extra research on the area. Again, this topic will be addressed in subsequent chapters.

There are some general pros and cons regarding the idea of a destination wedding. In our opinion, those pros and cons can be summed up in terms of the following:

Pros:

o   Complimentary Wedding Packages:

Many resorts offer an entire wedding package for free with a minimum night stay. This package also includes the services of a wedding coordinator who is assigned to helping you with all of your wedding plans. In addition, your wedding coordinator can usually help to organize activities for your guests.

o   Avoiding Stressful Family Interactions:

Typically a destination wedding would include a smaller invitation list, this way you would not feel obligated to invite random family relatives or friends that you barely know or just do not like. You can invite your close friends and family, or just have the two of you!

o   You may save money by having a smaller group:

Since you have a smaller group, your costs may be

much less than they would be with a large group, however the per person cost may be close to the same as what you would pay anywhere, plus, you may end up hosting additional activities that you normally would not with an at home wedding, so keep that in mind when planning – the cost may actually be a bit more expensive than what you planned.

o   Convenience:

You may choose to combine your wedding and your honeymoon by honeymooning in the same place you choose to marry. You may also want to think about returning to that exotic destination for anniversaries – how fun and romantic! Remember you do not always have to stay in the same hotel as guests, so you can arrange for some alone time if that's important to you. If you do decide to stay at the same hotel as guests, at least for the wedding weekend, you may want to plan on changing hotels and going to another nearby city or romantic hotel for some time after the actual wedding, therefore separating your time a bit. This may help you and your husband to feel as if you are enjoying a "real" honeymoon if you're staying in the same hotel with guests.

Cons:

o   Long Distance Planning and Legal Differences:

If you are not having a wedding coordinator, you will

have to work on quite a few details from a remote location. You also need to familiarize yourself with various legal requirements for marrying in potentially a different state or country.

o   Certain people may be unable to attend:

Some guests may not be able to attend your wedding! Guests may not be able to afford the expense, be able to take off time from work, or may have other obligations during that time. For older guests, it may be more of an inconvenience than anything. You may want to try gauge interest and availability with those important to you before making a final decision. Keep in mind that although some of your guests may be unable to attend, you may end up having more time to spend with the guests that actually do end up attending – therefore making it a more intimate affair. This is an important point to consider, in addition, just because some guests may tell you initially that they will be joining you, don't be surprised if that number shrinks when it is time to book!

4.3 Common Misconceptions

Misconception Number 1: Destination   Weddings are cheaper than at home weddings.

When we began planning, we thought that a destination wedding would be much less expensive than a wedding in our hometown. Truth be told, factoring in the at home reception, out of town gifts, all other incidentals, we spent a little bit more than we would have had we had the wedding at home. Destination Weddings may appear to be cheaper because you will most likely have fewer guests who are able to attend. However, on a per-person basis, you may not notice much of a difference. There is a chance though, that if you do not live in an expensive city, like Chicago or New York, it may cost you more to go to a destination than to stay at home.

Misconception Number 2: You can't have all the normal "wedding" activities you would in your hometown if you are marrying in a remote location.

You can do anything you want these days – a wedding is a wedding, regardless of where it is. If you want a specialty cake with multiple layers and flavors, you can have it done, regardless of where you are. If you want specialty flowers, music, etc... you can do pretty much whatever you want. A destination wedding can be as traditional or nontraditional as you want to make it.

Misconception Number 3: Even if I'm not getting married in the United States, the wedding planners that I work with in resorts will be just as responsive as if I were back home.

HA. A big HA. That's what we thought too.... until we realized what "Mexico" time was. Get used to a long response time, especially if your destination is out of the country. Things happen when they happen. It's important to note that if your destination wedding is not outside of the country you may not run into this issue as, in our opinion, this is probably more of a cultural difference between countries than anything else.

4.4 Budget

Okay, you have decided you want to spend your life together. Now it's time to let the planning begin. When Uriah and I first started looking into wedding plans, we didn't really know what we wanted or what we had to work with.

We think the first place to start, painful as it may be, is with the bottom line. What can you afford to spend? Now is the time to take a look at your budget, identify all parties that will contribute to your budget, and what items your budget will include.

Please refer to the table below for a sample budget. This budget should help in giving you an idea of most of the categories that will affect your final cost.

One thing I noticed while we were planning, was that we would start looking at the largest costs – the food and beverage tab, for example, and forget about how much all the other incidentals (gifts, flowers, invitations, etc.) add up. Don't be as naïve as we were. Know your budget, and know what ends up affecting your bottom line.

It is also a good idea to think about what percentage of costs go to what portions of the wedding. The sample budget below provides the general guidelines for this kind of breakdown.

Typical % of Budget	Description	Cost	Typical % of Budget	Description	Cost
50%	Reception		10%	Wedding Attire	
	Site fee			Dress	
	Catering costs			Headpiece	
	Bar & Beverages			Lingerie	
	Wedding Cake			Jewelry	
	Valet Parking			Shoes	
	Transportation to Reception			Hair/makeup	
	Service Fee (wait staff, bartenders, valet)			Groom	
	Rentals (Table, Chairs)				
	Decorations (Other than Floral)			Other	
	Other				
	Total		10%	Photography	
				Photography	
10%	Music			Videography	
	Ceremony			Engagement Pictures	
	Cocktail Hour			Wedding Package	
	Reception		4%	Stationary	
	Other			Invitations /enclosures	

Typical % of Budget	Description	Cost	Typical % of Budget	Description	Cost
	Total			Announcements	
10%	**Flowers**			Postage	
	Ceremony on site			Programs	
	Bridal Bouquet			Place Cards	
	Bridesmaids			Thank You Notes	
	Boutonnieres				
	Corsages - Mothers		6%	**Extras**	
	Reception flowers, centerpieces, cake table			Bridesmaids luncheon	
	Other			Attendants' gifts	
				Wedding gifts for each other	
				Favors	
				Wedding Rings	
				Rehearsal Dinner	
				Marriage License	
				Church fees	
				Officiant Fee	
				Assistant Fee	

You should also go a step further if you plan to have an at home reception – you will want to figure out what you feel comfortable spending on the at home reception budget versus the real wedding budget.

A key point when dealing with the budget is to remember that just because you have set an initial budget, you are by no means done thinking about it. Unless you have an unlimited budget, which nearly none of us do, you will be reminded of it every time you make a decision. You will certainly reach a point in your planning when something would cost more than you have budgeted. At this point, you have three choices:

1. Take money to pay for it from something else in your budget and sacrifice elsewhere. Be careful in doing this! Because we tend to plan things in sequential order, you may spend too much money during the beginning of the process only to realize you have run out at the end. For example, you will most likely pick a location before you worry about such items as transportation for your guests. You may find the location you love but realize it costs $2,000 more than you hoped to spend. If you go for it, promising to save elsewhere, you may end up having to drive your own guests back to their rooms after the reception!

2. Make sacrifices. Once again, unless you have an unlimited budget, I hate to say it, but you probably won't be able to get everything exactly the way you want it. You need to think about the budget as a whole and not focus on the individual items on their own. If you follow the approach we have outlined, you should be able to stay within these

guidelines while still feeling like you have control over the process.

3.   Increase your budget. As much as we'd like to think that this never happens, you may come to this point. Maybe you just didn't estimate well when you went through the process the first time. Maybe you went down the path of #1 too many times and now you have no money left over! Whatever the reason, be prepared to deal with this situation if you reach it. The worst possible scenario would be to get most of the way through planning, having put down deposits and all, and then have to panic to find more money. Always have a backup plan that you can pull out if the situation truly requires it.

Okay, so now you have your budget. One thing I think is critical to remember – you can do whatever you put your mind to it on a variety of different budgets. One girl I know had a wedding with 50 family and friends on the beach for only $3,000 for everything! Granted, she sent out electronic invitations and the ceremony and reception were at an all-inclusive, meaning the guests basically paid for their own dinner, but the point is...you can usually do more than you think you can with what you have, it is just a matter of being creative with your budget and your ideas. Remember the key point – this is all about what you want, so have fun with it!

4.5 What Kind of a Wedding Do You Envision?

The first thing you need to do before you plan any further is to determine what your wedding style is – maybe lots of guests, in an elaborate church affair? A small, intimate gathering?   Flashy bright lights in Vegas? A snowy, mountaintop ceremony? Everyone has a different style, and there is no good or bad decision – everyone is different so think about what is best for you!

My fiancé and I grappled with this question quite a bit when we first started – we went back and forth. We knew we were drawn to the whole wedding on the beach thing, but since we wanted to get married on the beach, would that mean we would have to go by ourselves? Was it rude not to invite certain people? In the end, we decided that for us, it just wouldn't seem like a wedding without at least a handful of close friends and family. We knew we didn't want to do anything too unusual, just a traditional style gathering on the beach.

We wondered about the extended guest list, and decided that many people probably wouldn't attend a wedding that was too far away, so we decided to base things on the 50 or so people we thought would attend. Once we had the decision made that we did not want to elope and marry alone, but that we also did not want to marry in Chicago and would want to invite guests with us, we were able to start looking at locations.

Before you are ready to move forward, ask yourselves the questions below. These should help to clarify your wedding needs/wishes and the type of wedding you envision for yourself – an elaborate affair with a huge bridal party and a large attendance, a quaint ceremony on the beach? Something familiar? Something culturally different like an authentic Mayan ceremony? The possibilities are endless!

Also – be sure to keep in mind that with a far-off locale, not everyone will be able to attend due to convenience or affordability – will this affect your decision making at all?

What kind of wedding is right for us?
Questions to ask yourself

Guests

- Do you want to elope and get married with only each other, or do you want to have your family and friends in attendance?

- How large is your guest list? Less than 50? More than 150?

- Will you be comfortable if some guests may not attend the wedding?

- Do you have any flexibility in your date? If you pick something close to the holidays, consider people's other obligations (family, etc).

Style

- How formal of a celebration do you want? Your options could range anywhere from a full plated dinner to a simple celebration with champagne and wedding cake.

- Do you want to do something traditional, or perhaps a more unique setting? You could get married on a beach, while bungee jumping, or on a cruise ship at sunset.

- Would you like to have an at home reception upon your return for those who are unable to attend the destination wedding?

- Do you want a religious ceremony only or a civil ceremony as well?

Planning

- Would you like to handle the details of the wedding yourselves, or would you like the assistance of a wedding planner/coordinator? This person may make things much easier for you by being familiar with your location.

- Are you willing to be flexible about elements of your wedding to save money and time?

- Is there a specific time of year, season, or date you want to get married?

- Do you expect to assist your guests with

any or all of their cost to travel? Attending a destination wedding can be a strain on a budget for many of your friends and relatives.

- If you have a larger guest list and your destination requires a flight, have you researched which airlines fly there? You may want to look into a group discount with your booking.

- If you are marrying outside of the United States, will all of your guests be able to obtain a passport?

4.6 Picking a Date

There are a few things to keep in mind when picking a date.

If you have your heart set on a beach wedding, but dream of getting married in September, you may want to think carefully about your location and timing. Hurricane season runs from May to November in the Caribbean, with the exception of those past the hurricane belt. Additionally, many other tropical locations have a rainy season during their winter. You should have a backup plan in case of rain regardless, but it's always good to lessen your chances!

Also – if you dream of having a winter theme wedding in December, keep in mind that this is right around the holidays – people have other standing travel arrangements/accommodations and may not be too excited to go places with other holiday travelers, increased prices, and full flights. You want to make sure that your date is convenient without causing increased travel hassle!

In addition, travel during your location's off-season is going to be cheaper, but there's a reason why not as many people are there. You need to decide which is most important to you – the date, or being able to afford and accommodate everything you want to do and having guests do the same.

4.7 Choosing a Destination

4.7.1 What to take think about when deciding where to go?

So you have set your budget, picked a date, decided that a destination wedding is the way to go for you, now let's start looking at various locations. Picking a location was, for us, the most difficult decision we had to make. It took so long, and was overwhelming and confusing. There are so many options out there!

In my mind "destination wedding" obviously has connotations of a sandy beach... merely because that was what our "destination wedding" was all about. A destination wedding could be a trip to Aspen to go skiing, a trip to upstate New York, a farm in the middle of the Midwest, or really, any type of location that is any sort of distance in relation to where you live.

The questions in the previous section (determining your wedding style) should help to narrow down the options as to what type of destination wedding you want to have. Once we decided we wanted a beachfront location, we took a few different things into account:

- **Budget** - We knew our budget, so we had a fairly good idea of what we were looking at for the ceremony and reception costs.

- **Guests vs. Eloping** – We had decided that we would not be eloping, so we would definitely want at least close family and friends to be with us.

- **In the United States vs. Another Country** – Although we would not be planning on paying for anyone else's accommodations (See Etiquette, Ch.18) we also knew that no one would be able to afford a far island like Tahiti, or a European destination like Santorini or Italy. We wanted to find something somewhat unique, but still accessible for guests. We could also have selected something on the coast of California or Florida, but we figured if people were paying for airfare anyway, we might as well go someplace that was a little more exotic than the US.

- **Ceremony/Reception Type** - We knew that we wanted a beachfront location, with a fairly informal but traditional ceremony.

These were, you could say, our initial criteria, so, off the bat, we had narrowed down our choices. We began looking at Mexico, and every island from the tip of Florida to the tip of South America, excluding Central America (we were already going to another DW there and did not want to follow suit).

I think everyone's initial decision criteria will be different; again, depending on what is important and right for you to make your day special. It's imperative to go through a thorough decision-making process up front, identifying potential risks and roadblocks. These initial decision criteria allowed us to narrow our results and get us closer to making a final decision.

Selecting a destination - Questions to ask yourself

Location

- Do you want to get married in the United States or somewhere outside of the country? You could go anywhere – Europe, a Carribbean island, or maybe Tahiti?

- Do you want to go to an English-speaking destination?

Weather and Timing

- What kind of weather are you looking for? Warm and sunny, some place where it never rains, a tropical rainforest, or the snowy Alps?

- What time of year is best to visit? You may want to think twice if the best time of year to visit is in November and December as this time of year may be inconvenient for guests.

- When is rainy/snowy/cold season?

- Has your destination been hit by recent bad weather: hurricane, tropical storm, or drought? Have facilities been affected?

- Do you want to be in a crowded area with other vacationers or somewhere more secluded?

Travel

- Do you want to go to a place you have been together before or experience a completely new city or country?

- How long does it take to drive or fly there?

- Is a drive required after flight?

- Can you save money by marrying during the off-season?

- Is your destination too remote? You will need to be able to have access to wedding services and planners, unless you plan on bringing your own from home. This includes a wedding planner, florists, caterers, photo- and videographers, and officiants.

- Does the destination offer lots of activities for pre- and post-wedding activities? You probably don't want your guests to be stranded in a location with nothing to do outside of the wedding itself.

Other

- What would you like best about the destination?

- What would you like least about the destination?

Legal Considerations

- Make sure you understand the wedding laws in the location you have decided on. If you're getting married in the United States, you may want to call the marriage license bureau at your destination. Find out what requirements or guidelines they have for making sure you can legally be married.

- If you are getting married outside of the United States, you need to be even more diligent. We offer some suggestions in a later chapter, but make sure you are well versed on the local laws and regulations before you decide! Some countries may have residency or medical requirements which may limit your options. Also, many countries outside the States will require extra paperwork as would be considered a foreign citizen.

- You will want to know if the wedding documents have to be translated or notarized and who can legally do this? Not everyone reads and thinks in English, so be prepared for extra work if going to a foreign country.

- You should find out how long they estimate it will take to process your paperwork. Some countries require a minimum stay in order to be legally married. You would hate for a technicality to ruin the best night of your lives!

Weather Information

- You should also check the weather in your locations – either ask someone at one of the resorts you are talking with or check the following websites for historical weather information:

- The Weather Channel:
  http://www.weather.com

- Weather Underground:
  http://www.wunderground.com

- You will want to find the average high and low temps and the times for sunrise and sunset:

- http://www.sunrisesunset.com

- You may also want to check out humidity, and the chance of precipitation. If you are getting married in the daytime, 80 degrees may seem perfect but not if there is 95% humidity!

4.7.2 Narrowing Down Your Results

So, based on the above list of questions, you hopefully have a list of various countries or states in mind. How do you narrow them down? You probably need to use whatever your main criteria are for the wedding itself and the location. It is helpful to keep coming back to these main criteria as you go through the decision making process, otherwise you will continue to go back on your decisions. Find the most important things for the two of you and continue to focus on those throughout the course of your planning.

For us, the most important items were the following:

- o Affordability for guests

- o Activities for guests

- o Tropical, beach Location

Your criteria may be in line with these, or you may be concerned about completely different things.

In order to narrow our list down even more, we went through the following thoughts:

I had previously traveled all over the Bahamas and the Caribbean, and, with the exception of Jamaica, while the islands are all fabulous, I was hoping for something a little bit more unique. We also wanted something that would be affordable for guests, and offer a bit more to do than the typical beach vacation.

We immediately decided that most of the US Virgin Islands were very expensive, and didn't have anything to offer that was very different from a lot of the other pretty islands in the Caribbean. With that in mind, we narrowed down our list to the Bahamas (mainly due to affordability), Jamaica (I had fallen in love on a previous visit), Aruba (very unique, far, and somewhat exotic), and Mexico.

We started looking at various hotels in these countries and it was hard to narrow down. It's so overwhelming just because there are so many different cities/hotels, etc.. to investigate.

Everyone's decision is different. What matters most is what you picture on your wedding day, the type of feel for the ceremony and reception. For us, being such travelers by nature, and for me, being somewhat of a sun worshipper, a seaside sunset ceremony captured the feel of the unique, perfect, romantic evening that we had in mind. All of these locations could offer the seaside ceremony that we desired, so our next criteria would really have to be affordability and activities for guests. My parents are in their 60's and 70's – they are not beach bums in any sense of the word – we really wanted to find a location where they would have other activities available to them than sitting out in the sun.

We researched vacation pricing in each of these areas, and realized that Mexico and the Bahamas were the most reasonably priced. We realized that in terms of activities for guests, Mexico beat the Bahamas hands down... It was in the heart of the Mayan ruins, boasted some of the world's best diving, beautiful beaches, shopping, golf courses, etc...

After months of lists, phone calls, emails, and research, we had finally narrowed down a country! How exciting! On to the next decision!

4.7.3 Making a Final Selection

For you - once you have decided on a country, and are narrowing down options for a city or a final selection, it will be helpful to make a list of pros and cons for each city. This will really help to outline your options in black and white. It may be a matter of shopping, or nightlife, of diving, whatever your main important items are, stick to them, and don't waver – you'll find what you are looking for.

For us, this was almost as difficult as picking a country - think of all the cities in Mexico – the beautiful sunsets the west coast cities of Puerto Vallarta and Acapulco have to offer, the fun nightlife in Cancun, the peaceful, European feel of the Mayan Riviera... Our options were, again, endless.

We loved the idea of a sunset wedding, but were drawn to the Mayan ruins, great diving, and tons of tourist attractions for our guests. We decided to go with Cancun, or Playa del Carmen – a great area for travel with beautiful beaches, renowned diving, and in close proximity to the Mayan ruins. It was really an area that had a great variety of activities and the beautiful beaches we loved!

As you can tell, to make the final decision, we had, again, come back to review those original three key factors:

- o Affordability

- o Activities for guests

- o Tropical Location

Once you know what you want and are unwilling to compromise on, the decision becomes easier, we promise!

5 Planning Trip

Okay – we had decided on a country, we had decided on a city, and we were narrowing down some properties, but as beautiful as every property looked, did we really want to marry in a place site unseen? No way!

If you can, I recommend going down for a planning trip – it will help you to further fall in love with the area, and get a better feel for what you want – the types of hotels you would like to look at, the ability to inspect different sites, various activities to plan for the rest of the weekend for guests, etc...

Even though you may be from Chicago, and it happens to be November, with a conveniently scheduled planning trip for the 80-degree sunny weather of Mexico in November, DON'T waste time. You are only in this area for a few days – you have your work cut out for you. Before you go, make an appointment with a wedding planner (if you have one), research and make appointments with various hotels or ceremony/ reception sites, and also take some time to investigate various activities or locations for rehearsal dinners or excursions for your group. If you are far enough in your planning, you may also want to select some specific vendors to meet with – taste cake, see florists, listen to bands.

Some of the resorts (especially All-Inclusives) may be closed to non-guests. It's amazing how many doors open once you are on these lists! Without an appointment it will probably be tough to get in and/ or tough to get the information that you are hoping to obtain. For us, it was helpful that, being fluent in Spanish, we were able to talk our way in past some of the gate guards, but even once inside, without an escort, we didn't have much to do and weren't provided much information on the wedding specifics for the resort. We were able to walk around and check out the location, but we really didn't have a feel for what options are available the way we did when we actually had a prearranged appointment and someone to take us around and answer questions.

You should definitely be prepared to take LOTS of photos and LOTS of notes of places – they all tend to blend after one or two. Definitely make a list of what you liked and didn't like about each place, it helps you compare your choices when you are done with your visits and hopefully helps drive to a final decision.

A good thing to keep in mind is to check out stores for gifts or items you may want to use while planning – check out postcards to use as possible Save the Dates, t-shirts, anything that captures the local flavor.

As I mentioned above, you may also want to schedule activities you are thinking of planning for your guests so that you can check them out before hand (sunset cruise, snorkeling trip, etc.).

Now is a great time to go through the process of experiencing anything you may need to in order to feel more comfortable about the activity or place given the remoteness of your planning.

Regardless of what type of venue you choose to marry at (Ship, All Inclusive Resort, Non All Inclusive Resort, Villa, B & B), the following questions should help with your initial planning research.

Don't be shy in asking questions while visiting or interviewing potential places over the phone! You are the customer and are entitled to have everything the way you want it. Don't be intimidated by wedding planners or hotel managers who may try to push you into specific packages. It is clearly in their best interest to sell you on as many incidentals as possible, some of which you may want, but don't be pushed into buying something you don't.

If in doubt, go with your gut feeling - you don't need to stick around in a situation where you don't feel comfortable. We toured a couple of hotels during our planning trip and knew right away that they were not the right places for us. In one situation, the hotel manager had gone out of his way to give us a complete tour of the grounds, offering champagne while we rode around on a golf cart. While this was appreciated and we certainly weren't going to turn down his offer, don't let yourself be swayed into making a decision by overlooking what you really are after. If you stick to your questions and know what you are looking for, you should be fine.

Planning Trip/Site Inspection – Questions to ask

Packages/Pricing

○ Does the location offer honeymoon and/or wedding packages?

- Most locations that we looked at offered a discount of some sort for honeymooners or newlyweds. If you stay at the same hotel where you hold the ceremony or reception, you may typically get your room for free or an upgrade the night of your wedding. In addition, some places may offer a free wedding package with a certain night stay. You should look into this type of an option – you may be able to save a few thousand dollars.

○ What are the different wedding packages and what is included in each? Use the checklists that we provide below to make sure you are covering everything that you need. Don't forget to throw in some extras for yourself, if you can afford it, like a candlelit dinner or a pre or post wedding massage!

o If an option is not included, don't be afraid to ask! Don't forget that you are the consumer and the location is here to cater to you, although it is easy to be swayed into something you may not be crazy about and get overwhelmed. Just stay prepared!

   • Be weary that some places may advertise a wedding package for a cheap price, but it is very generic. They will then try to tack on "extras" like flowers, music, etc. and before you know it you are paying more than you would at a competing location.

o If there are no packages, how are weddings priced? According to the number of guests?

   • Some hotels charge an extra fee if you don't have a certain numbers of guests staying at the resort. This number could range from 1 room to 20 rooms, from our experience. You may be required to book a number of rooms yourself on your guests' behalf to guarantee a specific rate.

o What kind of a deposit is required to hold your date? Typically a location may charge between 10-30% to "hold" a date.

o What are the payment options for the deposit and subsequent payments?

   • Never pay for anything in cash – even if you get a receipt you have no way to challenge charges or payments made. Always pay with credit cards wherever possible, and always get everything in writing!

o   If getting married at a specific location, is the honeymoon included free of charge in the package? Larger hotel resorts such as all-inclusives, or cruise ships generally offer this amenity. Other locations may also offer this if you ask!

o   Many hotels, resorts and cruise ships understand the importance of return customers. If you plan on making a return trip in the future for your anniversary, see if they offer any discounts. Recently, the Waldorf-Astoria hotel in New York offered special anniversary rates of 80-90% off the rooms for couples who were married 50 years before, with proof that a wedding or honeymoon was held on site.

Timing

o   Does the destination have your desired wedding date available? Do you have a backup date in case yours is already booked?

    •   Regarding legal requirements, make sure you understand how far in advance of your wedding day you must arrive. This is typically at least 2-3 days in most locations.

o   How many other people will be marrying at your destination on that day?

- Some of the larger all-inclusive hotels that we looked at had multiple weddings in the same day. Nobody wants to be pushed out of their own wedding for running over, but this is a very real concern that you need to think about. This may be no different than getting married at a popular church location back home.

Logistics

- Does your location use an on-site wedding coordinator? Will that person be there on your wedding day or are they just there to make your initial planning easier?

  - Is there an extra charge for this coordinator?
  - How easy is it to get in contact with this person once you are home from your planning trip?
  - Do they have their own direct phone number or will you have to contact them via someone else (front desk, etc.?)

- How much paperwork will you have to process yourselves? By hiring a wedding coordinator you typically would have them process most of your paperwork and arrange a meeting with the local marriage bureau. Are you comfortable handling this alone if not working with someone locally?

- If selecting a set package at a resort, hotel or cruise ship, how much flexibility do you have in selecting extras? Do you get to compare menus, bands, flowers, photographers, etc?

o   What are the options for bad weather/change of venue?

o   Can you meet the officiant before the ceremony? Can you choose the wording of the ceremony? Can you personalize your vows?

o   Can you hear tapes of bands? Will the resort/ ship guarantee in writing that this is the band that will play (ditto for photographers)? Where can you get married on-site? Is anything off-limits? What happens if it rains?

o   Many locations offer themed or pre-decordated weddings. Are these for you? How much do they cost?

o   Is your location accustomed to handling a wedding with your number of guests? A smaller hotel may not be able to handle a group of 200 – make sure you ask those questions ahead of time.

o   How will you make sure your paperwork is properly received back home? If working with a wedding coordinator, will they mail the forms back for you? Do you need to arrange to pick them up yourselves?

o   How late is the site available? Some hotels may have time limits on the amount of time available for the ceremony/reception. Additionally, the location may have a curfew at night – if you plan on partying late you may have to move elsewhere. Ask ahead of time!

Guests

o   Can the location give references from couples that have had weddings in the past?

- This is important especially if you have an unusually large party – destination weddings tend to be smaller in size and a location may not be able to handle large groups.

o   Is there a limit on the number of guests who are allowed to attend the ceremony? Does the resort charge a fee for non-guests?

- Some of the all-inclusive hotels that we looked at were adults-only, and children were not allowed on the property under any circumstances. Others allowed children for the ceremony and reception only. Others may have had sister resort properties that allowed children if theirs did not.

o   If you expect everyone to stay at the same location, does the hotel/resort have enough rooms available for you? What are their options if they can't meet your needs? Perhaps a sister property is available which could handle overflow guests.

o   If booking a large number of hotel rooms, does your location offer group discounts?

o   Depending on the type of reception you decide to have, can your hotel handle it? Almost every location can handle a small group for cocktails and appetizers, but a large seated dinner may be a different story.

- Can you see the locations where these would be held? What are the ranges of prices per person and can you customize the menu?

6 Picking a Hotel/Ceremony/ Reception Location

There are many different types of hotels or facilities to look into when planning on marrying in another country. When we went down for our planning trip, we weren't really sure what we wanted – it really helped to be able to go down and check things out for ourselves.

You should definitely compare event facilities and, if you're wedding at a hotel, or on a ship; room amenities, activity options, and group discounts.

Be mindful as you're planning – especially in the Caribbean, a lot of these hotels fall into one of three categories: couples only, adults only, or family friendly. Be aware of your guest list and have alternate options available for those that may fall outside of the rules of the place you are booking at. Do any hotels have a minimum number of rooms that need to be booked before you can wed there? Do you have to pay a fee for guests not staying at the hotel?

You should also ask for pictures of any ceremonies and receptions held at the resorts. There really is no substitute for seeing what other weddings before you have done, it makes the comparison so much easier. For example, one of the locations we looked at was in the process of setting up for a wedding that afternoon, so we were able to see how they handled both the ceremony and the reception. The ceremony was set up on a pier, which looked small from a distance, but once we took a closer look, there was easily space for 50+ guests and a large aisle down the middle. If we hadn't been able to see the set up I would have never guessed that more than 20 people would have comfortably fit. You also get a good feeling for the style of what the location has to offer, and the first impression is usually the correct one, and the one that remains with you.

(Take a look at the section above, Planning Trip, for additional questions and things to think about and keep in mind when picking a location).

7 Where to marry? Ceremony ideas and types

This all comes down to personal preference – do you want to be married in a church, by a priest of one denomination, two priests of differing denominations, or do you want to have a nondenominational service? Whatever your wishes are, just be sure you ask the right questions in your destination city.

Where ever you may be, you can either have set vows or choose to customize the vows (if you are provided this option). There may also be rules in regard to witnesses in various countries. If so, you may want if the resort would provide witnesses if necessary. You may want to request to meet with the officiant ahead of time, either before the ceremony itself or on your planning trip.

You should also clarify (if you will be marrying in a foreign speaking destination) what language the ceremony will be in. There may be an extra charge to have an English speaker translate for you.

8 Reception Details

There are a few different options for receptions – do you want a champagne and cake reception only? Appetizers and hors d'oeuvres? A full seated lunch or dinner?

Do you want guests to pay for their own drinks? Do you want a full open bar? With an open bar, do you want to pay by consumption or just charge an hourly rate for guests? Unless you have a very heavy drinking crowd, you will probably be better off paying per drink, if the site allows such an option.

Asking the questions below will hopefully allow you to gather enough information to make a reasonable decision on what type of reception options you will want to look into.

Planning the reception – Questions to ask

Decorations/Space

- How will the reception be decorated? Can you see pictures from previous receptions that have been held there?
- Can I select my own colors for the decorating?
- What areas may we have a reception at? What is the size for each? How many guests can be accommodated without a problem?

Costs

- What is the per person cost? Don't forget to break this down into the component costs – appetizers, meal, and drinks.
- Is there an additional cost to rent out the space?
- Can you send me sample menus for various options?
- What is the charge for drinks? Cash bar? Based on consumption? Open Bar?
- Do you offer a hurricane guarantee? What is the plan for rain? If an outdoor location, is there a place indoors that you can move to and still be able to accommodate the number of people you have?
- Is entertainment provided?
- Is there a separate dance floor available?
- Do you offer alternate menu items for guests with special needs, such as kosher or vegetarian options?

8.0.1 Wedding Packages

Although you may be looking at different types of venues, regardless of what they are (ship, B&B, hotel, all-inclusive), you will find some pretty standard types of wedding packages across the board. There are typically three types – the Yugo, the VW, and the Rolls Royce. They can range in price from $700 to $3000 depending on where you choose to go and what package you select. Here are some examples of what you may find:

Standard Package:

- o Consultation with wedding coordinator
- o Minister/judge provided
- o Processing of legal documentation and assistance with document translation
- o Small wedding cake

Upgraded Package:

- o Consultation with wedding coordinator and minimal services
- o Location site fee/ceremony setup
- o Bridal bouquet and a boutonniere
- o Music (prerecorded)
- o Photography with minimal number of photos
- o Champagne Toast
- o Small wedding cake
- o Minister/judge provided
- o Processing of legal documentation and assistance with document translation

Deluxe Package:

- o Consultation with wedding coordinator and minimal services
- o Location site fee/ceremony setup
- o Transportation to/from ceremony
- o Bridal bouquet and boutonniere, flowers for attendants
- o Music (prerecorded)
- o Photography – upgraded package
- o Champagne Toast
- o Small wedding cake
- o Minister/judge provided
- o Processing of legal documentation and assistance with document translation
- o Wedding album and video
- o Pampering for bride and groom

Add-Ons:

- o Some or all of these items may usually be added on to your package.
- o Local Band, DJ
- o Live music during ceremony
- o Add-ons to flowers, photos
- o Reception
- o Additional decorations

*Note that gratuity is not typically included in any of the above prices, however it is usually a set rate between 10-20%.

8.1 All Inclusives

An all-inclusive hotel usually has reasonably priced food/beverage plans for groups of people. Many of these can be huge resorts. Some may have additional costs for guests not staying at the resort to attend your wedding.

You should be sure to verify all elements that the wedding package includes at these resorts. Are there any items that you would have to pay additionally for? Also, some AI may have multiple weddings per day, and there may be a minimum night stay required to book the wedding. It is helpful to know these things in advance.

Many hotels (not just AI) have various location options available to you for your ceremony and reception – be sure you ask about the min/max number of guests for each and their location.

You should also ask how the venues are decorated – some decorations may be included, some may be additional out of pocket costs to you.

There is also a large subcategory to this group that the Sandals, Couples, and Superclubs resorts belong to. These large properties cater to weddings and have popularized the term "Weddingmoon". They usually have a set wedding coordinator, and free wedding packages based on a minimum night stay. They also do multiple weddings a day so, with all other resorts, just be sure to ask the right questions up front in order to find out if these properties are right for you.

8.2 Non-All Inclusives

Non all-inclusives are just typical hotels that don't have food/beverage options included in the package price. This is a nice alternative if you are in a nearby city that has great nightlife or entertainment – that way you can explore the area and get out of your hotel for meals.

8.3 Boutique Hotels

Boutique hotels are typically smaller, more unique hotels – they can also come with a hefty price tag. On our planning trip, the hotels we most fell in love with were boutique hotels. They all seemed to be very quiet, not crowded, and have deserted stretches of beach, very conducive to private weddings. If you can afford it and want to spend the money, I would go for this option. One problem you may run into with a smaller boutique hotel is that if you have a large group, you are basically renting out the entire place and this will obviously add significantly to your cost.

8.4 Alternate Ceremony/Reception Locations

8.4.1 Villas

You can also look into renting a private villa or condo. This is a nice option if you want to have a somewhat secluded beachfront ceremony where onlookers will be minimal (unless you are near the main hotel drag or zone in your destination city). If you plan on making your vacation longer than the typical weekend wedding, this may definitely be a good route to consider.

One thing to be weary of with villas is that you will typically have to rent them out for an entire week. While the daily price may be cheap, by the time you have paid for a seven day rental you will easily have spend a couple of thousand dollars.

With a villa you will also need to remember that you may have less services than with a hotel or all inclusive resort. Maid and chef service may be included, but you may also be obligated to clean and cook for yourself! Make sure you ask the right questions before exploring this option. If cooking for yourself, make sure there is a grocery store nearby, etc..

Finally, if you are thinking of getting married at a villa, don't forget to account for the additional cost and facilitation of potentially having to utilize multiple vendors for your event such as various companies for set up of the ceremony site, tents, caterers, staff, etc.... It may take a bit more time and planning with this option so be sure to be thorough with your research, planning, and budgeting!

8.4.2 Restaurants

A restaurant is another good option for a secluded ceremony/reception (provided you are able to rent the location out or have a private room).

You really want to do your research on all of these – if you can come up with off the beaten path info from locals, you will be better off finding a good deal!

Restaurants are similar to boutique hotels – in some cases, you will be paying a hefty fee for privacy and/or brand. The restaurant may be giving up a lot of business that night in order to host your wedding and they want to be compensated accordingly, especially if it is a well known establishment.

8.4.3 Bed & Breakfasts

A bed and breakfast is a quaint alternative to a larger hotel – it may behoove you to make sure that they have been utilized for weddings in the past, and make sure that your vendors are do not anticipate any problems with the space.

8.4.4 Cruises

Many cruise ships now have on-site wedding coordinators familiar with wedding legalities at the many ports of call for their ships, allowing them to offer you their opinions of the best ports to marry in. Some ships also have onboard wedding chapels. A very unique and fun way to tie the knot!

You should also ask if the cruise line has any wedding planner affiliates in specific ports of call, and what the various packages are.

8.4.5 Wedding Chapels – Vegas Style

Some areas such as Las Vegas, Nevada boast a variety of small/medium sized wedding chapels – if this is one of your dream locations you should ensure the seating threshold works for your guest list, find out the types of ceremonies they may offer, and info about any wedding packages they may have.

When selecting a site, you should find out if the site is private, and, where the closest hotel or public area is. If privacy is a concern and the area is public, you can ask if the site may be closed for your use only.

9   Should I work with a Wedding Coordinator?

A wedding planner local to your destination or a travel agent specializing in booking travel for destination weddings can be a very important investment towards ensuring that your special day goes off without a hitch. Because you will not be in your hometown and you will be unaware or unsure of all the area has to offer, it may benefit you to work with a wedding consultant in the area. The consultant can help to find and oversee local vendors, and make sure that things happen as they should.

If you've signed up for a wedding package, the services of a planner are probably included in your package. If you haven't, you might want to think about putting aside some of your budget (about 10% of the total) for a wedding planner, especially if you are marrying in a foreign country where English may be a second language. You coordinator will be able to research and secure local vendors, and will also be responsible for creating gift bags for guests, greeting everyone at the airport, keeping people busy with fun activities once there, addressing special requests (babysitters, dry cleaners, etc.), and getting everyone where they need to be on time.

We decided to attempt to do our planning ourselves, and then after running into many roadblocks, decided to go with a wedding coordinator. This is all a personal preference – I just wanted to feel comfortable knowing that someone was available to handle all of the details we would need to coordinate, in addition, since our group wasn't all staying together, and we wanted to plan additional activities, we wanted everything tied together.

Prior to going with a wedding coordinator we made many calls ourselves, and ran into problems – it took people a long time to respond, sometimes the language barrier was an issue. We thought it would be easier for us to have a wedding coordinator located in the area to coordinate vendors and do a lot of the calling and back and forth that we were running into problems with.

Do keep in mind that just because someone is local, this does not necessarily mean that they will have any less of a problem obtaining information about certain locations or from vendors, especially if you are planning in a different country – expectations are just different.

It is smart to do your homework too and fully research your wedding coordinator by asking the appropriate questions before you provide them with a deposit.

Make sure you feel comfortable, and your gut tells you it is right before you move forward.

We have heard horror stories from girls that moved forward with wedding coordinators, only to find that their coordinator was less than helpful, and also dishonest! One girl had a request for a certain officiant, she let her coordinator know one year prior to the ceremony, and then after one year of planning the girl was told that the officiant was booked. The girl emailed the officiant – he said that the coordinator never even contacted him! In this instance, it was a matter of personal interest – most wedding coordinators may make money by sending their customers to certain referrals. It's unfortunate, but it does happen quite often. In order to avoid issues such as these, be sure you ask for referrals and information about your wedding coordinator before you contract their services. In addition, take a look at the questions below.

10 Should I work with a wedding coordinator? Questions to ask

Experience

o   How much experience does the wedding coordinator have with your destination?

o   Can you get a feel for how many weddings the coordinator has been a part of? How many of them have been for groups from out of town? Have there been any couples from your immediate area that you could call for reference?

o   Does the consultant have sample photos of weddings that they have planned? Solid references or testimonials?

Costs

o   How does the wedding coordinator determine their rates? Typical rates are either by the hour, or by the package. If you plan on customizing many of your options, you may be better going with a flat fee up front so you can factor the cost into your bill.

- o What is the fee to start the process? Is there a deposit? What are the payment methods available? You should always pay with a credit card wherever possible, never in cash.

- o Can you get an initial estimate of cost from your coordinator? They will typically ask you for a budget to help put a framework around initial discussions.

Logistics

- o Beyond planning the wedding, is your coordinator able to plan travel for your guests and yourselves? What about setting up honeymoon accommodations? You may be required to use a travel agent in addition to your on-site coordinator.

- o How can you communicate with this person? Via Email? Phone?

- o Will this person attend the ceremony?

- o Is this person easily accessible?

10   Selecting Vendors and Vendor Relations

Hopefully you are lucky enough to be working with a wedding coordinator to help you pull everything together, but in the event you are not, and you must hire your vendors without meeting, be sure to ask for a portfolio of pictures and at least two references. The references should be from an event that is comparable is size and event-type to yours.   For example, a reference from a bar mitzvah for 10 people doesn't help if you're planning a wedding for 50. Also ask for the names of other vendors who worked those events to check as further references regarding the company in question.

It may be beneficial to think about sending hand-written thank-you notes to personalize your interaction with this company or individual.   During the event itself, you should always keep in mind that tipping is usually acceptable, especially in foreign countries and at resorts.

Another option you may want to think about is to bring your own vendors – if you can afford it, fly in companies that you trust from home for certain things that may be extremely important to you such as photography, hair/makeup, lighting, and flowers.

10.1 Selecting a Photographer

This is just personal opinion, but, if you're trying to cut costs, I would not recommend using the photographer as a place to start.

We had decided that we would be in such a far away place for a once in a lifetime event, and, with only a small group of people to actually experience the event we wanted our pictures to capture everything from the time we were there. Now, if you have friends that are experienced in photography, you may want to save money and also feel comfortable having them take your shots. We didn't, but that is our personal opinion.

Otherwise, when comparing photographers, be sure to ask the following questions:

Selecting a photographer – Questions to ask

o   What are your packages and promotion, if any?

o   Will you provide a CD of photos, and how long before we may see the photos?

o   Can you provide a sample of your work that has been done in the past?

o   Will you provide negatives? (If not doing digital photos)

You should also plan on having a list of 'must have' shots you want to take. It is most helpful to have samples of these so that you can show your photographer what you need, and you may also want to arrange to meet with the photographer before the wedding.

Your wedding day will be frazzled so you want to do your research beforehand and let your photographer or wedding planner know the shots you want to have taken. How sad would you be if you completely forgot the types of shots you wanted to capture that day and lost the opportunity to capture those moments forever?

10.2 Selecting a videographer

The process to select a videographer will probably be similar to that of selecting a photographer.

You can ask the following questions of the videographer to get a better feel for what he/she may offer:

o   What packages are available – are they with music or without, what length, etc.?

o   What format can we purchase the video on? DVD and/or VHS?

o   What style does the videographer use? (It will help to see samples, while reviewing, note the look, sounds, and quality of the images)

o   How old is the equipment and what is the editing process? Ask for clarification on any areas that may seem unclear to you. Remember, the whole point is to get the memories that you want, not what someone else thinks you want!

o   Generally, what is your overall feeling with the videographer? You will probably want to make sure you feel somewhat natural around this person!

10.3 Entertainment

When deciding on the kind of entertainment to have at your event, you will most likely want to think about the group that will be attending (mostly younger people with hip tastes in music? An elegant crowd that would appreciate the sounds of a big band instead?) Keep in mind what your guests are interested in as well as what you and your fiancé like most! In addition, it may be a fun idea to capture the feel of the area – for example, a reggae band if you will be in Jamaica.

Take a look at pricing for both a band and DJ.... Try to balance the pricing with what you are more drawn toward. If you go with a DJ, be sure you provide a song list and let them know anything you do not want played! Same thing with the band – also, ask for sample tapes if you'd like!

11 Attire

As I have made mention of in most every chapter thus far – you can be as traditional or nontraditional as you would like – this goes for the attire as well.

Want a traditional ball gown? You can go ahead and wear one – just keep in mind if you are having a ceremony on the golf course in August you may regret your decision later! Would you rather do something more laid back? No tuxes or even jackets for the men? Go with whatever suits your style.

Your fiancé may opt to wear something linen and comfortable, or a light jacket and slacks, some may even choose to wear shorts and hawaain shirts. Or if you are marrying in a cold place you may prefer to have a fur wrap along with your dress!

It is also perfectly acceptable not to wear shoes if you're having a beach wedding, in fact, it may be hard to maneuver in the sand in any sort of shoes! Keep in mind the location you will be in and the tone (formal/informal) of your wedding.

You should also think about how you want your guests to be dressed – many people choose to put this type of information on their websites (casual attire, no shorts), etc...

By all means, this is all yours to decide! There are no rights or wrongs here!

12 Guest Lists – How to invite and Who to invite?

One of the toughest things we grappled with was how to handle the invitations. Of our list of 140 people, we knew only about 50 or so would be attending our destination wedding. With that in mind, who to invite and how to invite them?

We wondered if it would be rude to invite all guests when we knew only a portion would be able to attend? Would it be just as rude to not invite certain guests because we knew they wouldn't be able to attend? Would we send an announcement to the others? How would we handle an at home reception?

You can handle this a few different ways. One option, what we decided to do, was send a save the date to our entire list, along with an invitation to everyone. On our response card, we offered the option to select attending an at home reception (we added date and time). See sample (Appendix 1). We also invited everyone to the shower as well.

Now if you aren't hosting an at home reception, you may want to think about handling this is a different manner. You could send invitations to your close friends and family that would be attending, and announcements to the other group of people.

Another option would be to send separate invitations for each reception (destination and at home reception) for each group of guests. Whatever you feel comfortable with and works for you and your fiancé is appropriate.

If you are having a planned elopement, you may want to send an announcement/invitation to at home reception in one mailing (see example Appendix 1)

Always remember, even though it's hard not to take it personally, don't be upset if some of your closest friends or relatives don't attend. While you may be paying for some of the food and activities for the weekend, their fees for airfare and hotel can certainly add up, and it is understandable if they are not able to make it.

One thing that we noticed was, while many of our friends were very excited and ready to go to a destination wedding, some of our parents or relatives from older generations seemed almost put off by the decision. Be prepared to be a big salesperson if you need to, and if some of the guests still cannot attend, you can't take it personally.

Tip: When you are sending out your invitations, be sure to number your RSVP cards with the guest they are addressed to – some people forget to write their names on the response card and this will make your life easier if that happens!

13 Save the Date

You should think about informing your guests about your plans as soon as possible – this way they can begin to think about budgeting for the trip and making their travel arrangements.

We decided to send a save the date magnet, along with a newsletter containing various information and our web address about nine months prior to the wedding. Our newsletter (see sample, Appendix 1) contained the following information:

- o Intro and reasoning behind having a destination wedding
- o General information about the area and it's location
- o List of websites with information about the destination
- o Flight pricing
- o Information on documentation needed to get into and out of the country (if it is an international location)

- o   Weather
- o   Currency conversion information
- o   Languages spoken
- o   Hotel options (if you have this information yet)
- o   Nearby attractions
- o   Our wedding website

Something like this will be helpful in getting your guests excited about the trip along with providing them some helpful information to start their planning.

You might want to think about whether you want coordinating save the dates to match the theme of your invitations, although, if it is early in the planning process it may be too difficult to select these upfront.

14 Planning a weekend/Hosting Multiple events

If your guests are going to be around for a few days in your wedding destination location, you should keep a few things in mind.

One – you are their only contact once they reach the destination – you should be prepared to field questions about anything from medical concerns to special activities and city highlights. It may be smart to provide some information to the group upfront or assign one of your attendants to be the point person for guest concerns.

Two – While it is very nice to plan various activities for people to attend as they wish, be sure that no one feels obligated to attend. Remember, many guests have shelled out big money for this trip and they may want to utilize this time for some much needed R & R for themselves and their family. We will be attending a destination wedding and plan to treat it as our own much needed personal vacation in addition to a celebration for our friends. Chances are, other guests will do that too.

14.1 Multiple Events – Things to Think About

You can either plan a wedding weekend in the destination, or plan a full week (five or seven days) for people to stay. You may also want to think about staying in a resort away from your other guests so you and your fiancé can have some quiet time together away from the group.

You will want to think about when you will be hosting your activities and what types of activities they will be. Is your wedding going to be on a Saturday or another day of the week? If people are going to be around all week you may get better rates on pricing if you select a wedding date other than Friday or Saturday. In addition, the chance for multiple weddings at your venue may be reduced. If guests are already planning a lengthy trip anyway, it shouldn't be much of an inconvenience.

It can be challenging to come up with activities for a weekend long celebration or a weeklong celebration. Once again, don't feel obligated to have to plan things just because people are going to be there – your wedding coordinator, if you have one, should be able to help out with this by at least providing a loose schedule of potential activities in the event you do not want to have a planned group activity.

It is nice to have an open agenda of activities to offer your guests including both things that are native to the area, such as a luau in Hawaii, and things that are just popular for the group – golf, for example. Make sure that all activities you are thinking about cover a range of prices – be sure to include some inexpensive alternatives if the majority of events may be pricey. You should determine ahead of time which events you would hope most guests would attend (the wedding for example), and keep others open without the expectation of guests attending (a golf get together, perhaps?)

Be able to offer all relevant information about the activities up front - if there are any fees, if children can attend, etc.

One other thing to consider is that many all-inclusive resorts may offer many activities for free with the resort package. This may include such things as day trips, scuba diving, snorkeling, etc. Make sure to ask if you are hosting the events at an all-inclusive.

If you're having a website, it's great to note this information there so that guests have an idea about potential activities before the trip!

14.2 Rehearsal Dinner

You may want to think about the city that you are marrying in – are there other cities nearby that may be fun to experience while everyone is in the area? Would you rather have the dinner at the same location as the wedding? (Sometimes this is easier if you are staying at an all inclusive).

Do you want to have something that is a little different than what a rehearsal dinner would normally be – something that captures a feel for the local life? A sunset catamaran cruise? A luau?

Are you interested in something formal or informal? Would you rather have cocktails and appetizers or a full dinner? Do you plan on inviting all of your guests or just family and those in the wedding party?

One of the unique things about a destination wedding is that typically everyone will be an out of town guest. This changes the rules of etiquette to the point where it is probably correct to invite everyone to some sort of event beyond the wedding, such as the rehearsal dinner. As such, it doesn't necessarily have to be quite as formal as a typical rehearsal dinner may be if you held it back at home.

15 Planning Guest Travel

Finding group rates for airfare and hotel will be very much appreciated by your guests, and sending travel info is a nice gesture too.   You should never feel obligated to pay for any of your guests travel costs though.   Of course, it is very nice if you can afford it, but it is not necessary, although some couples will pay for their bridal party accommodations.   Once again, go with what you feel comfortable with. If you need to reserve a group of rooms at your hotel in order to secure your rate you may end up being obliged to book a few extra rooms just to ensure you reach your minimum.

If you are inviting friends and family, you may want to look into low cost options such as all-ages, all-inclusive resorts or cruise during low season (generally May through November at resorts in the Caribbean or Mexico), to keep costs down and provide many different activities for your guests.

15.1 Working with a travel agent

Travel agents can help to make all of your guests and your own planning much easier than it would be if you did it on your own. Also, they can shop around to find you the best deal so you don't have to, as well as coordinate the different legs of your trip (i.e. – transportation to and from airport in addition to booking airfare and hotel). You also may be eligible for good rates based on group bookings.

Selecting a Travel Agent – Questions to ask?

- o Is the agent familiar with your destination city, and have they stayed at any of the resorts they are recommending to you?

- o Does the person have any experience working specifically with destination weddings?

- o You will also want to find out how the travel agent charges a commission and what type of travel insurance they recommend for the trip.

  - • Trip cancellation insurance typically allows you to recoup the entire cost of your trip in the case of an emergency. See if it is an option that the travel agent offers, even if you don't necessarily take it.

- o Ask for a 24 hour emergency number that is accessible from any country – you do not want to be in a rut with no one to reach if you happen to run into problems on your journey, it is also a nice thing for your guests.

- One thing that people don't realize is that you typically cannot call 800 (toll free) numbers in the US from outside of the country. This is more of a problem in Europe than it is outside of North America, but be prepared just in case.

15.2 Airfare

It is obviously beneficial to research group discounts once you find out the main airlines that travel to your destination. If you're not working with a travel agent, you can quickly do research on this on a main travel website like Expedia, Travelocity, etc. Do keep in mind that these websites may not necessarily offer you the best rates. With airfare becoming very competitive these days, many airlines are offering the best rates through their own websites, including specials not offered anywhere else. As with everything, it pays to shop around and look for the best options!

Another option would be looking at chartering flights, not a blue-sky idea when you look at all of your guests that will be attending. This option is much more feasible when all of your guests are leaving from the same location though. You may have to fly guests to one location first and then catch a charter flight from there. Be careful if you do this that you leave enough time for people to arrive – flight delays are common and you would hate to leave people behind!

It is also important to find out if tickets are refundable, and what the penalty is for changes.

15.3 Hotel Bookings

Based on your guest list, you will want to try to work within the parameters to find out about group discounts at various resorts. For example, if all of your guests have children, then a couples only resort would be out of the question unless there was a sister property that was child-friendly. Likewise, if most of your guests are singles, you wouldn't want to waste time looking into a couples only resort.

Are the hotels you are looking at nearby to your wedding location? If people are all over the place, this might make a difference in your transportation costs.

There is also usually one main hotel where most guests stay – you can let people choose their own, but be sure they understand they may be far from the locations of all of your hosted activities.

While we didn't want everyone to feel obligated to stay at the same hotel, we wanted to ensure that people were somewhat in the nearby vicinity. With that in mind, we decided to recommend 3 hotels to people to stay at based on a variety of budgets. If your location is nearby or has a sister city, it may be nice to offer one of your hotels there. If transportation is an issue, you could look into having a shuttle or car pick up the guests that are staying at the out of the way hotel at least for the ceremony.

At whichever hotels you decide, you will want to find out the following information:

Booking hotels – Questions to ask

o How many rooms are needed to group rooms for a discount?

o What is the discount?

  • What are the cancellation rules?

o What type of deposit do I need to put down to guarantee the block?

o Does the hotel have any minimum stay requirements?

o What is included in the room rate? (Breakfast, airport transfers, etc.)

o If the hotel is in another country, do they offer US-based electrical outlets? Many foreign countries use different voltage systems but offer converters or have dual plugs. If not, you will need to purchase an adapter before leaving home.

o Does the hotel offer a frequent stay/rewards program?

  • If you are booking a large group of rooms for your guests, you might as well take advantage of it and see if you can get rewards points. If you are not in a frequent stay program you can usually sign up for one on the hotel's website. It could earn you free rooms for the future!

15.4 Transportation

If your location is far from the airport (Negril, Jamaica, is about 2 hours from the Montego Bay airport for example), it would be very nice to arrange for transportation for your guests. Of course, if people are coming in at various times this may not be a possible.

Many hotels and resorts will offer an arranged shuttle service for guests, especially in foreign countries. The last thing you want your guests to do is have to flag down a taxi in an unknown country and worry about whether or not they get to their hotel successfully.

16 Wedding Party

As destination weddings can be as traditional or nontraditional as you want them to be, so can your wedding party. Don't want one? Forget about it. Do you have 3 bridesmaids and no maid of honor? Who cares?

We had four bridesmaids, one best man, and two groomsmen. I didn't want to pick! Do what works for you and your fiancé. Just be sure to tell your bridal party about the destination before you ask them to stand by your side so that they can decline if they are able to make it. Destination weddings can be seen as unaffordable and inconvenient for some!

I put together a little gift package to send to my bridesmaids (only two were in my hometown) to ask if they wanted to stand up with me. I had purchased four mini sombreros on our planning trip. I added a matching Mardi Gras bead necklace, a mini toe ring (in the shape of a flip flop), tropical lip balm, and a message in a bottle with a note. This allowed them to have some time to think about it without me standing over their shoulder, and a unique way to incorporate some local touches and the beach theme while asking.

17 Planning the Honeymoon

If you are already in an exotic location, who needs to go anywhere else for the honeymoon? You may want to think about staying in your own resort and vacationing for a longer time than your guests if you opt to do this. Chances are you'll save money and also enjoy it!

We opted to have our honeymoon in Tahiti after our wedding in Mexico – we wanted a more exotic destination and we new we would probably never set aside time to travel there otherwise.

Don't forget to include the cost of the honeymoon in your budget! Some people consider their honeymoon a separate vacation and plan for it as such, but you would hate to get to the end and then have to scale bck on honeymoon plans because of poor budgeting. The honeymoon is the perfect place for you to get away nd escape with your new husband/wife and you don't wnt to be worrying about aything, espeially ony

18 Etiquette

One thing that we have learned most in this process, time and time again, is that there really does not seem to be a right and wrong – with the advent of destination weddings, people really tend to do whatever feels right for them and their pocketbook.

I would recommend purchasing a wedding etiquette book for all of your etiquette questions, but I would feel free to honor the guidelines loosely – for what is most suitable for you and your fiancé, your event, and your budget. Below I jotted down some items that we had questions about, a wedding book specific to etiquette concerns may be more helpful to you.

18.1 Who pays for what?

Guests should pay for all of their own expenses with the exception of the wedding party. It used to be that the bride or her family should traditionally cover hotel for the bridesmaids; the groom or his family should do the same for the groomsmen.

If people are unable to afford to pay for accommodations for their bridal party, it is typically understood, that is why it will be important that your bridal party knows where the wedding will take place so that they may plan accordingly. It does help if you insist they not buy you gifts. It is a large commitment for people to travel to a new destination for your wedding, and it's not appropriate to expect gifts in addition to the expense of travel. This goes for all guests attending, not only those in your bridal party.

18.2 Tipping

Tipping is usually not included in your costs for the big day, so if you don't have to worry about it the day of, you may want to appoint someone to handle the tipping responsibilities. Be sure to plan accordingly and have labeled envelopes for each recipient. Typically the best man would take care of handling these duties but this may differ depending on your situation.

You should talk with the manager at your venue as well as your vendors to determine what the tipping policies are beforehand (some venues include the tip with the total on the bill). Don't be afraid to ask.

The personnel that may be included in the service charge are the following:

o **Banquet Manager:** If gratuity is not included in your bill total, about $200 to $300 for a tip is reasonable, depending on the size of your wedding.

- **Caterer & Wait staff:** Determine the tip according to the number of waiters -- decide on a dollar amount and multiply by the number of waiters.

- **Bartenders**: About 10% of the bill is fine.

- **Hair, Makeup & Nails:** Tip as you would normally, about 15% to 20%.

- **Wedding Coordinator:** A thank you note or gift is a nice gesture

- **Officiant:** The tip should be between $100 and $200. You should also expect to feed the officiant.

- **Transportation:** About 15-20% is customary

- **Parking Attendants/Valets**: About $1/car

- **Coatroom and Restroom Attendants**: If this gratuity is not factored into the bill already, $.50 to $1 per guest is fine

- **Musicians (ceremony and reception):** Optional, but if you do $20-30 per musician.

- **Photographer/Videographer:** This is optional, but $20 to $25. You should also expect to feed the photographer.

Again, be sure that gratuity is not included for any of these services, and also be sure that you are pleased with the services themselves. If not, you should never feel obligated to tip anyone!

18.3 Gift Registry & Shower

The whole idea of registering for gifts was one that we grappled with from the time we got engaged and started discussing the destination wedding idea. I didn't feel that it was appropriate to have people buy gifts for us when they are spending quite a bit of money just to make the trip down to Mexico to watch us marry.

At the same time, people wanted to buy us gifts and wanted to celebrate with us in that manner. As one of my friends so eloquently put it "you better register otherwise you are going to get ugly gifts that you don't want and can't use!"

In the end, with us having an at home reception too, we felt a little more comfortable about the gift giving process, so we did register and we did allow people to throw us showers.

Do what feels write for you – there is no right or wrong.

18.4 Inviting Guests to other activities

You may wonder if it is appropriate to invite guests to showers or celebrations if they are not attending your wedding and are not even invited.

We had a hard time with this, and, in our opinion, if someone was not invited to the wedding, they should not be invited to a shower either. It may be ok to invite some of your girlfriends or other men to your respective bachelor and bachelorette parties, because the expectation for providing gifts is not there, but that decision is up to you.

Of course, many people may still want to shower you with gifts, so do what you feel is right. For us, we didn't feel it would be appropriate if we hadn't been hosting an at home reception.

You may also question if it is ok to invite guests to an at home reception if they are not invited to the destination wedding itself. In our opinion this is Ok – it allows them a chance to celebrate with you upon your return.

18.5 Out of town gift bags

Even if your destination is local to some people but they are staying in the hotels anyway, if you plan to provide out of town gift bags for out of towners staying at the hotel, you should provide out of town gift bags for everyone.

You may want to think about providing your out of town gift bags to guests or bridal attendants prior to your departure – that way you have less to carry or worry about, although, it may be more difficult for them.

In addition, if you are working with someone trustworthy at a resort, or a wedding coordinator at your location, you may want to ship the bags to your destination.

19 Nice extras

You may want to make sure that each guest has a
passport or be able to provide them with information
on how to get one. Be warned that the turnaround
time for a passport can be up to 6 weeks, so warn
people not to wait until the last minute!

In addition, sending a save the date card or newsletter
with information about your wedding and the area is a
nice gesture (see template, Appendix 1).

Setting up a wedding website is helpful, you can look
into a few different hosting companies for this:

Wedding Window: http://www.weddingwindow.com

Wedding Channel: http://wedding.weddingchannel.com

EWedding: http://www.ewedding.com

Another nice gesture is to place a gift basket in each
room that is full of nice to haves for the trip (suntan

lotion, bottles of water, maps of the area, etc.) and also various items that will remind them of the setting – bottle of tequila, samples of native food, or crafts from local stores.

If you have a small group, you also may want to incorporate a "who's who" with the gift basket so that everyone has a bit of background on the other guests attending the wedding and subsequent events.

20 Planning tools/tips

The following are a few extra tools and tips that we've incorporated to make things easier for you!

20.1 Workbooks

I was a bit lost when I initially started planning, even a lot of the books/magazines I ordered had things that weren't conducive to the continual, detailed tracking that I prefer ☺. I chose to utilize a variety of different templates to come up with my own unique workbooks in Excel to help me manage my wedding info. These worksheets are available via CD-ROM and include the following:

- ○ WEDDING TIMELINE
- ○ ITINERARY TEMPLATE
- o SAMPLE RSVP RESPONSE CARD WORDING
- o SAMPLE WEDDING BUDGET
- ○ ELECTRONIC WEDDING PLANNER
- ○ PLANNING TRIP INFORMATION TEMPLATE

- PLANNING TRIP ITINERARY TEMPLATE
- PLANNING TRIP SUMMARY TEMPLATE
- 'DAY OF' ITINERARY FOR WEDDING PARTY
- GUEST LIST MANAGER (For both AHR and DW)
- SAMPLE SAVE THE DATE NEWSLETTER

Please see Appendix 1 – Additional Templates and Resources for further information

20.2 General Information – Where to start?

The web is a wonderful thing. Start with a search engine like Yahoo (http://www.yahoo.com) or Google (http://www.google.com), and the possibilities are endless. You can find out all of the following on the web – in fact, we did MOST, if not all, of our research on the web:

- You can find info about various countries/cities to find which is right for you.
- You can find all info about legal wedding requirements in various destinations.
- Message boards are a helpful resource to share tips and garner opinions.
- A wedding website is very helpful for those with Internet access to post info about your big day.
- Be sure to be sensitive to those folks that may not be as Internet savvy as the rest of us. Great Aunt Alice may appreciate having the information sent to her in paper form.

Here are some of the websites we found most helpful:

- o The Knot.com (http://www.theknot.com) – This was my favorite, hands down – a great resource, helpful ladies, and interesting articles.
- o UltimateWeddings.com – (http://www.ultimateweddings.com) This was a close second
- o Chicagoweddingpages.com – (http://www.chicagoweddingpages.com)
- o Weddingchannel.com – (www.http://weddingchannel.com)
- o Chicagobride.com – (http://www.chicagobride.com)

21 The week of the wedding

Be sure to plan to get into town at least a few days before the wedding itself – this actually may be mandatory in some countries for the ceremony to be legal. You can also ensure that necessary paperwork has been filed and arrange for any last minute details to be addressed.   Most importantly, you will be well rested and relaxed by the time your wedding day arrives.

Be prepared! There is a common feeling that something will always go wrong at a wedding – just look at all of the moving parts that need to fit together perfectly for things to go off without a hitch. You can minimize any potential disaster by doing what you have been the entire time – being prepared and knowing how things are supposed to play out. If you know what to expect from all parties involved, there should be no big surprises.

22 Last but not least – 14 Extra Hints

1.   Be sure to confirm all agreements in writing!
      The last thing you want is for something to
      go wrong at the last minute and not have any
      written verification on what was agreed to.

2.   Pay for everything with a credit card only –
      never use cash!

3.   Don't forget – This is your wedding – you get to
      make the rules – go barefoot, wear a sundress,
      do whatever you want!

4.   Dress for the location – a huge, satiny, drapey,
      silky wedding dress may not be a smart move if
      your climate is 90 degrees and humid. Sweaty
      is not sexy.

5.   Brides – Book your hair and makeup in advance,
      and do a trial run if possible. With all of the
      last minute plans and logistics going on, don't

forget about your pampering! (If you plan to do your own hair, be sure to check first on the electrical current and plugs at your destination. You may need to bring converters for hot rollers and other appliances.)

6. You may want to think about bringing an extra duffle bag for any gifts received, or arranging for a family member to take them home for you if you are going to be honeymooning for some time.

7. Know your itinerary and have a copy with you. Leave copies with family and friends.

8. You should also be prepared to carry all of your original documents--including birth certificates, passports, and divorce papers, if applicable--in your carry on. Never pack these in checked bags either! Make copies of your passports to leave with family and friends and suggest that your guests do the same.

9. Keep your travel emergency number with you at all times.

10. Keep all confirmation numbers with you at all times.

11. If you're getting married in a wedding dress, you'll definitely want to carry it with you – would you trust checking it? We all know how things can happen. Most airlines will let you hang a garment bag in a coat closet. Even if there is only one in First Class and you are seated in

coach, you can ask the employees at the check in desk and also the flight attendants when you board the plane. Most people understand and are happy to help!

12. Grooms should hold on to their clothing too just to be on the safe side. Unless you make specific plans before hand, you may be surprised to find that on the islands things are a bit different – it won't be as easy to find a tuxedo rental shop for your use!

13. If you are in a warm locale, you may want to think twice about giving candy as a favor – it may easily melt!

14. Don't be surprised if family and friends are not 100% supportive of your decision. If this is what you and your fiancé want, have a talk with those that you are concerned about...if this is still a problem – you need to do some serious thinking about what is right for you. While this decision is about the two of you, you should still be considerate of the feelings of those close to you.

23 Planning an At Home Reception

When you decide that you want to plan an at home reception in addition to the other events that you will be hosting, it will be helpful to go back to section 4.5 to ask yourself the same questions about what type of an event you envision. You will probably find that your answers to these questions will change for your second celebration.

If you went all out planning your destination wedding and events during the wedding weekend, you will most likely not have the resources or interest to go all out for a follow up at home reception. You may find that if you opted for a sit down dinner in your destination, you will choose appetizers and drinks only for a second celebration.

In addition, you should think about photography – will you want someone to capture the moments? Will you want an additional videographer? Florist? Will you need additional gifts and place cards? What about a cake? You may find that you end up paying for the equivalent of two weddings due to all of these extras.

Your bridal party, and you and your fiancé – do the two of you plan to wear your wedding attire? Is your bridal party expected to attend both gatherings (not an issue if everyone is in town, but can be quite costly for those that are not in town)!

You will probably want to revisit your budget once you decide what you want to do for a second party and possibly even have two budgets to keep all costs tracked.

Definitely plan on showing the wedding video and pictures at the reception at home for those that were unable to attend – they'll appreciate it!

24 Destinations and cruise info – Popular ones and ways to obtain info

24.1 US Destinations

Below I have listed some popular US wedding destinations and links to a few sites to help you out with some initial information.

Because you would be marrying in the country, the legal requirements wouldn't be as difficult as a wedding out of the country, but there are differences from state to state – do your research.

- o Las Vegas
  – http://www.weddingslasvegas.com
- o Lake Tahoe – http://www.weddingstahoe.com
- o Disneyworld – http://disneyweddings.go.com
- o Key West – http://keywest.com
- o Nantucket Island, MA
  – http://www.nantucketweddings.com
- o Napa Valley, CA – http://www.napavalley.com

o   Hawaii – http://www.wedhawaii.com

24.2 Cruise Weddings:

Major cruise line info:

o   Carnival – http://www.carnival.com
o   Disney Cruises
      – http://www.disneycruise.com
o   Holland America
      – http://www.hollandamerica.com
o   Royal Caribbean
      – http://www.royalcarrribbean.com
o   Princess Cruises – http://www.princess.com
o   Windjammer Barefoot Cruises
      – http://www.windjammer.com

24.3 Foreign Destinations:

Here are a few other tips to keep in mind while planning to go to a foreign destination:

Under U.S. statutes, a marriage performed abroad that's valid under the laws of that country is generally accepted by any state. Some countries have a varied rules/required documentation that can vary by district or city, even judge!

Here are a few of the most popular destination wedding locations. Please see Appendix 1 for their legal requirements:

Caribbean:

Anguilla:
MORE INFO: www.gov.ai

Antigua:
More Info: www.antigua-barbuda.org

THE ISLANDS OF THE BAHAMAS
MORE INFO: Bahamas Ministry of Tourism, (888) NUPTIAL, or http://www.bahamas.com

BARBADOS
MORE INFO: Ministry of Home Affairs, (246) 228-8950, or http://www.barbados.org/weddings.htm

BELIZE
More Info: www.**belize**.gov.bz

BERMUDA
MORE INFO: Bermuda's Registrar General office, (441) 297-7709 or -7707; the Bermuda Department of Tourism office nearest you; or http://www.bermudatourism.com

BRITISH VIRGIN ISLANDS
MORE INFO: BVI Registrar's Office, (284) 494-3701 ext. 5001/2/3; BVI Tourist Board, (800) 835-8530, or http://www.bvitouristboard.com

CAYMAN ISLANDS
MORE INFO: Cayman Islands Government Information Services, (345) 949-7900, or http://www.caymanislands.ky

U.S. VIRGIN ISLANDS
MORE INFO: USVI Division of Tourism (800) 372-8784; Territorial Court, St. Thomas and St John, (340) 774-6680; Territorial Court, St. Croix, (340) 778-9750; or http://www.usvitourism.vi

JAMAICA
MORE INFO: Jamaica Tourist Board, (800) 233-4582, or http://www.jamaicatravel.com

MEXICO
MORE INFO: Mexico Tourism Board, (800) 446-3942

PUERTO RICO:
MORE INFO:

ST. KITTS & NEVIS
MORE INFO: stkittsnevis.net

ST. MAARTEN
MORE INFO: Office of Civil Registry, (011) 5995-22457

EUROPE:

ENGLAND
MORE INFO: Visit Britain, (800) 462-2748; British Consulate General, (212) 745-0200; or http://www.britainusa.com

SCOTLAND
MORE INFO: Visit Britain, (800) 462-2748; British Consulate General, (212) 745-0200; or http://www.britainusa.com

South Pacific:

FIJI
MORE INFO: Fiji Visitors Bureau, (800) 932-3454, or http://www.bulafiji.com

THAILAND
MORE INFO: U.S. Embassy in Thailand at fax (011) 66-2-205-4103 or http://www.thai-la.net

GREECE
MORE INFO: Greek National Tourist Organization, (212) 421-5777, or the Greek Consulate, (212) 988-5500

HAWAII
MORE INFO: Hawaii's Department of Health marriage licensing office or (808) 586-4544; or http://www.gohawaii.com

ITALY
MORE INFO: Italian consulate nearest you; the Italian Government Travel Office, (212) 245-5618; the local U.S. Embassy or Consulate in Italy, www.usembassy.it

25 Conclusion

Whew.... You certainly have your work cut out for you, but hopefully this book will help you to put some sort of a structure/methodology around your decision making process. Hopefully it has provided you with helpful information you can utilize while planning your ideal destination wedding, and provided some insight.

We've tried our best to use our experience in planning our own destination wedding to organize our thoughts, experience, and opinions for your benefit.

Have fun and good luck!

26 Appendix 1 – Additional Templates and Resources

Throughout the course of planning, I would run into templates and lists here and there – to track guest lists, gifts received, RSVPs, budget, etc... While I found some very helpful items, what I found most helpful (I am on the computer most of the day and evening), was taking a few good ideas from various samples, adding my own ideas, and creating my own. This was especially helpful for items specific to a destination wedding such as RSVPs for the at home reception, additional expenses (out of town gift bags), etc.

If you are interested in utilizing some of the same templates, I have a CD-ROM for sale with the following items:

- o WEDDING TIMELINE
- o ITINERARY TEMPLATE
- o SAMPLE RSVP RESPONSE CARD WORDING
- o SAMPLE WEDDING BUDGET
- o ELECTRONIC WEDDING PLANNER

- ○ PLANNING TRIP INFORMATION TEMPLATE
- ○ PLANNING TRIP ITINERARY TEMPLATE
- ○ PLANNING TRIP SUMMARY TEMPLATE
- ○ 'DAY OF' ITINERARY FOR WEDDING PARTY
- ○ GUEST LIST MANAGER
- ○ SAMPLE SAVE THE DATE NEWSLETTER

Please send an email to destinationwed1@yahoo.com for additional information.

In addition, Uriah and I are available for wedding consultations or planning services, send an email to destinationwed1@yahoo.com for services, pricing, and availability.

26.1 Wedding Timeline

This timeline includes information relating to a traditional wedding, and extra tips for a destination wedding:

SIXTEEN TO NINE MONTHS BEFORE WEDDING

- ○ Announce your engagement, take engagement photos if desired
- ○ If you want one, have an engagement party
- ○ Arrange for your parents to get together
- ○ Begin envisioning/discussing your wedding style and format and choose a date
- ○ Research various destination options
- ○ If you can select ceremony site and contact officiant
- ○ Send Save the Date cards letting everyone know the destination as soon as you have it

narrowed down so that guests and attendants may begin travel plans and budgeting for the expense

- o Setup a wedding website, if you plan on having one (also think about a newsletter for those without internet access)
- o Determine size of the guest list for an estimated head count
- o Determine your budget and division of expenses
- o Pick the ceremony site and meet with the officiant
- o Find a reception location and make reservations early
- o Interview wedding planners if using one
- o Interview caterers if using one
- o Purchase/create wedding planner (or use my templates to assist)
- o Purchase magazines/planning books
- o Check out websites, magazines, books for ideas

NINE TO SIX MONTHS BEFORE WEDDING

- o If you have selected your location, familiarize yourself with the legal requirements to wed there
- o Research accommodations for guests
- o Register for gifts
- o Shop for your gown
- o Choose your wedding party, and make sure they are aware of your expectations
- o Register for gifts
- o Hire wedding planner if using one
- o Finalize date and time for ceremony and

reception
- Finalize guest lists
- Choose a color theme
- Choose attendant's dresses
- Book your caterer
- Book your photographer
- Book your videographer
- Plan ceremony and reception music – interview DJs and Bands
- Compile names and addresses for guest list

SIX TO FOUR MONTHS BEFORE WEDDING

- Select a florist
- Order your gown – make sure your order contains the correct info and all of your questions have been answered
- Shop for cake
- Book your DJ or band
- Order invitations (think about wording and design beforehand) and party favors, response and thank you cards, announcements, and maps – You will want to send these ASAP if you are marrying away from home
- Negotiate group room rates
- Shop for bridal party tuxedos
- Schedule dress fittings
- Finalize arrangement for the church and ceremony
- Make transportation arrangements
- Plan honeymoon; visit travel agencies, make reservations
- All deposits should be made and contracts signed – reception, vendors, etc...
- Plan wedding decorations; decide which

packages you want to go with and what customizations are necessary

- Complete guest list – Assume 20% will not attend
- Finalize your travel plans
- Verify passport and/or visa requirements for travel
- Review document translation or other legal requirements for location
- Start planning rehearsal dinner
- Shop for wedding rings
- Attend pre-marital counseling

THREE MONTHS BEFORE WEDDING

- Choose gifts for attendants, parents, and helpers
- Buy wedding rings
- Order the wedding cake
- Buy cake knife, toasting glasses, guest book & garter
- Purchase and engrave wedding bands
- Make sure attendants have purchased dress and accessories
- Consider specific ceremony decorations, like a huppah, aisle runner, or other decorative elements.
- Pick out or design a ketubah or other marriage contract required by your religion.
- Determine songs for First Dance, Father/Daughter, Mother/Son, entrances and cake cutting
- Finalize music lists including must play songs and the do not play list
- Determine list of must take shot for

photographer, including which formal pictures are to be taken
- Finalize rehearsal plans

TWO MONTHS BEFORE WEDDING

- Make plans & reservations for wedding rehearsal & dinner
- Reserve rooms for out-of-town guests
- Address invitations/announcements
- Invitations should be sent 4-6 weeks prior to wedding; announcements after wedding
- Meet with officiant to finalize ceremony info
- Arrange for all insurance policies to include you and your future spouse (health, auto, homeowners, life)
- Get a name change kit or forms from the DMV, Social Security, credit cards, etc., if you are planning on changing your name
- Buy guest book
- Determine program details for ceremony
- If customizing vows, finalize these
- Thank you notes for items received at shower

ONE MONTH BEFORE WEDDING

- Finalize and confirm details of every aspect of your wedding (paperwork, airline tickets, hotel arrangements, flights)
- Create out of town gift bags and attendant gifts

- Have gown pressed
- Make sure you have garter, something old, new, borrowed, blue

- o Confirm honeymoon reservations
- o Have final fittings for you and your attendant's dresses
- o Get marriage license
- o Ask a friend or relative to take charge of guest book at reception
- o Pick up wedding rings
- o Purchase gift for fiancé (not mandatory!)
- o Create a packing list of all potential items for trip
- o Finalize seating for reception

TWO WEEKS BEFORE WEDDING

- o Prepare wedding announcement to send to newspapers
- o Contact guests who have not responded
- o Make any necessary appointments for beautification prior to ceremony for yourself and your attendants
- o Make place cards
- o Plan any additional activities
- o Plan toasts to friends and family

ONE WEEK BEFORE WEDDING

- o Pick up your gown, attendants' dresses & accessories
- o Confirm details with all participants and inform them of any changes
- o Pack for honeymoon
- o Make sure you have all wedding attire, rings & marriage license
- o Have rehearsal and dinner
- o Have nails done
- o Give final guest count to reception facility or

caterer
- Get a massage

UPON ARRIVAL AT DESTINATION

- Meet with wedding planner and discuss any additional decisions or details
- Leave out of town gift bags with concierge at various hotels
- Place fees due on the wedding day in envelopes
- Appoint a member of the bridal party to transport cake knife, toasting glass, and other heirlooms to and from wedding site

WEDDING DAY

- Don't forget to eat
- Have hair & make-up done
- Take marriage license and rings to ceremony site
- Begin dressing two hours before ceremony is to begin
- Mail wedding announcements
- Give wedding bands to those needed for the ceremony

Post Wedding

- Within two months of your wedding, set aside some evenings to write that stack of thank-you notes (together!)
- Write and send thank you notes to vendors who may have been particularly helpful – it's good karma and an appreciated personal gesture

26.2 Itinerary Template

This may be helpful to provide to your guests so that they are aware of the schedules of all of your various guests and activities.

Bride & Groom's
Wedding Week Itinerary

Est Time	Category	Details	Who	Time	
				Hrs	Mins
Day 1 - Tuesday 11/2					
9:ooam	Travel	Mona and Uriah arrive	Bride and Groom		
1o:ooam	Travel	Guests 1-4 arrive, flight #			
11:ooam	Travel				
12:oopm	Travel				
Day 2 - Wednesday 11/3					
1o:ooam	Golf Outing	Meet at Bus Stop in front of	All	4	
2:oopm	Lunch	Meet at Restaurant	All	2	
Day 3 - Thursday 11/4					

26.3 Sample RSVP Response Wording

You may want to get creative here, for example, if you are having a beach wedding, do you want to reference that? A ski wedding?

___ Save a spot on the beach for me

___ Sorry, I can't make it

Food selection would be included.

You may also include RSVP responses for an at home reception:

___ I'll be there with my new skis

___Sorry, I can't make it, but will be in Chicago!

___Yes, count me in for both!

___Sorry, I can't make either!

26.4 Sample Wedding Budget

This is part of the excel workbook. Each page comprises of a specific breakdown of costs and all are totaled on the main page.

The workbook is comprised of the following tabs:

- Wedding Coordinator

- Ceremony Setup Costs

- Reception Costs

- Wedding Attire

- Wedding Cake

- Music

- Flowers

- Transportation

- Gifts

- Parties

- Photography

- Videography

- Miscellaneous

In each section, there is a breakdown of costs, such as the following, for Stationary costs:

- Invitations

- Response Cards

o   Reception Cards

o   Inner Envelopes

o   Seating/Place Cards

o   Maps/Directions Cards

o   Ceremony Programs

o   Save The Date Cards

o   Announcements

o   Thank-you Notes

o   Stamps

o   Calligraphy

o   Matchbooks

o   Personalized Napkins

There is space for a typical amount of spend, what you have budgeted, and what you actually spend.

The front tab of the workbook is a summary tab of each of the worksheets, so when you enter your actual spend on the correct tab, it is automatically added to the summary page and added to the total running costs.

26.5 Electronic Wedding Planner

An excel workbook that includes all your necessary items to keep you organized. Tabs/worksheets include the following:

- o Timeline (from section earlier – includes notes and status section so you may track each item)

- o Vendor Contacts page

- o Generic Contacts Page

- o Sample Song List

- o Expenses

26.7 Planning Trip Information Template

An excel spreadsheet that allows you to track the following information for your planning trip:

- o Hotel Name
- o Comments
- o URL
- o Rates
- o Suitable for wedding
- o Suitable for guests
- o Desire to see (rank 1-4)
- o Details
- o Appointment scheduled?
- o Wedding planner name
- o Wedding rates
- o Wedding on the beach?
- o Kids allowed?
- o Jacuzzi in room?
- o Max. guests
- o Cost for additional guests?

26.8 Planning Trip Itinerary Template

This is a color coded itinerary that allows you to space out your planning trip with all of your contact names, numbers, and addresses – scheduling out your day appropriately.

Time	Contact Name	FRIDAY – 12/3 Resort Name	Address
12:10		Arrive Airport	
1:00		Check – In – Hotel	
2:00			
3:00	Contact Name/Number	Hotel #1 (City #1)	
4:00		Hotel #2 (City #1)	
5:00			
5:30		Hotel #3 (City #2)	
6:00			
6:45	Contact Name/Number	Hotel #4 (City #1)	
7:00			
7:15		Ferry over to	
8:00– 11:00	No set appointment	Hotel #5 (Island)	
11:30		Ferry back to - SLEEP	

26.9 Planning Trip Summary Template

A helpful template that will allow you to compile all of your info from your planning trip into one format

Hotel Name: HOTEL NAME

Rank: #1

First Impression:
Breathtaking lobby with view of water and pool. Quiet, secluded, very expensive

Wedding coordinator:

Met with – Sales coordinator – she was lovely – very well spoken, friendly, lots of ideas

Wedding Area:
Pier area is great! Also – the beach is large and somewhat private – the hotel has a small, open, intimate feel

Cocktail area near spa would be on grass – this is OK. Restaurant is half open/half closed and bar and dancing would be outside later. Great layout

Rooms are amazing – each one is themed for a different country – so lush, large, luxurious

Overall:
Our very favorite

Rank:
#1

26.10 Day of Itinerary for Wedding Party

This includes a detailed breakdown for organizing your entire wedding day and bridal party!

BRIDE		GROOM	
TIME	**ACTIVITY**	**TIME**	**ACTIVITY**
9:00	Bride - HAIR		
	Mom - HAIR		
9:00	Bridesmaids drop stuff	9:00	Groom wakes from dreaming about his bride!
9:30	Bridesmaids arrive at		
9:45	BM #1 - HAIR		
10:00	BM 2- 5 - HAIR		
10:30	BRIDE, MOH, MOB - MAKEUP		
11:00	Bridesmaids dress	11:00	Dad takes Dave to Groom family arrives

26.11

Guest list Manager

	Guest List Manager						Total Attending	2		
		Total Meat	1			Total Vegetarian	0			
Side	Groom	STD Sent:	2/4/2005	Total Seafood Invite to shower?	1	Attended shower?	Y			
Name(s)	Tom and Sherry Smith	Shower Gift Received:	Pans					Thank You sent	2/4/2005	
Address	123. West Road									
	Chicago, IL	Invitation Sent		RSVP Rcvd	Y	# Coming	2			
	60614	# Invited	2	Table #	3					
Telephone:		Meat	1	Seafood	1	Vegetarian				
Email:	123@yahoo.com	Gift Received						Thank You Sent		
Relationship	Groom 2nd Cousin	AHR Invite Sent		RSVP Rcvd		# Coming				
Placecard name?	Same	# Invited		Table #						
		Meat		Seafood		Vegetarian				
Accommodations	Hotel Monaco	Gift Received						Thank You Sent		
	Arrival 11/2									

26.12

Sample Save the Date Newsletter

This is written in word, and set up to print on the front/back of a sheet with newspaper columns (three) and generic heading information such as the following:

- Bride and Groom's guide to <insert destination>
- Where is the location? <insert map>
- Where do we stay?
- How far is the location?
- What is the weather there?
- What is the currency there?
- What do I wear?
- What is the language?
- What is there to do in the area?
- What is the electrical circuit used?

27 Appendix 2 – Legal Requirements for various locations

(From theknot.com)

Anguilla:
RESIDENCY REQUIREMENT: Two Days
NECESSARY DOCUMENTS: Passports or certified birth certificates and photo driver's license; proof of divorce or death certificate of former spouse/s, if applicable.
MORE INFO: www.gov.ai

Antigua:
RESIDENCY REQUIREMENT: 15 days, unless you do a special license for a 150 dollar fee
Necessary Docs: Valid passport, or birth certificate and valid ID picture: e.g. driver's license or state issued ID, divorce decree if applicable or death certificate if widow
NOTE: Both parties must apply in person, and both must be over the age of 18
More Info: www.antigua-barbuda.org

THE ISLANDS OF THE BAHAMAS
RESIDENCY REQUIREMENT: 24 hours
NECESSARY DOCUMENTS: Passports; birth
certificates; proof of divorce or death certificate
of former spouse/s (if applicable); declaration
certifying both parties are unmarried U.S.
citizens, sworn before a U.S. Consul at the
American Embassy in Nassau; a marriage license
from the Commissioner's Office on other islands;
proof of arrival in the Islands of the Bahamas.
NOTE: Both parties must apply in person.
MORE INFO: Bahamas Ministry of Tourism, (888)
NUPTIAL, or http://www.bahamas.com

BARBADOS
RESIDENCY REQUIREMENT: None
NECESSARY DOCUMENTS: Passports or certified
birth certificates; proof of divorce or death
certificate of former spouse/s (if applicable);
letter from officiant performing service
NOTE: Both parties must apply in person
at Ministry of Home Affairs in Cheapside,
Bridgetown.
MORE INFO: Ministry of Home Affairs, (246) 228-
8950, or http://www.barbados.org/weddings.htm

BELIZE
RESIDENCY REQUIREMENT: 3 Days
NECESSARY DOCUMENTS: Passports or certified
birth certificates; proof of divorce or death
certificate of former spouse/s (if applicable)
More Info: www.**belize**.gov.bz

BERMUDA
RESIDENCY REQUIREMENT: None

NECESSARY DOCUMENTS: Passports and a "Notice of Intended Marriage" form from Bermuda's Registrar General's Office (The form is available by phone request or at http://www.bermudatourism.com. Fill it out and mail it along with a cashier's check or bank draft made payable to the Accountant General, Hamilton, Bermuda, in the amount of US$210 back to the Registrar General. Your license will be valid for three months and can be picked up at the Registrar's office by you or a designated person.)
NOTE: "Notice of Intended Marriage" must be filed 2 weeks before the wedding
MORE INFO: Bermuda's Registrar General office, (441) 297-7709 or -7707; the Bermuda Department of Tourism office nearest you; or http://www.bermudatourism.com

BRITISH VIRGIN ISLANDSRESIDENCY REQUIREMENT: None
NECESSARY DOCUMENTS: Passports or certified birth certificates; proof of divorce or death certificate of former spouse/s (if applicable)
NOTE: Publishing banns may be necessary for church weddings. Make plans with appropriate clergy.
MORE INFO: BVI Registrar's Office, (284) 494-3701 ext. 5001/2/3; BVI Tourist Board, (800) 835-8530, or http://www.bvitouristboard.com

CAYMAN ISLANDS
RESIDENCY REQUIREMENT: None
NECESSARY DOCUMENTS: Passports; birth certificates; proof of divorce or death certificate of former spouse/s (if applicable); return or

ongoing tickets; proofs of entry (Cayman Islands International Immigration Department pink slips or cruise-ship boarding passes); letter from authorized officiating marriage officer
MORE INFO: Cayman Islands Government Information Services, (345) 949-7900, or http://www.caymanislands.ky

U.S. VIRGIN ISLANDS
RESIDENCY REQUIREMENT: None
NECESSARY DOCUMENTS: Driver's licenses or passports; proof of divorce or death certificate of former spouse/s (if applicable); letter accompanying application for marriage stating date of visit, length of stay, and preferred wedding date if having ceremony performed by a judge
NOTE: Application must be received at least 8 days prior to wedding.
MORE INFO: USVI Division of Tourism (800) 372-8784; Territorial Court, St. Thomas and St John, (340) 774-6680; Territorial Court, St. Croix, (340) 778-9750; or http://www.usvitourism.vi

JAMAICA
RESIDENCY REQUIREMENT: 24 hours
NECESSARY DOCUMENTS: Certified copies of birth certificates that include father's name; proof of divorce or death certificate of former spouse/s (if applicable)
NOTE: Application must be made in advance of trip by calling the Ministry of National Security at (876) 906-4908. MORE INFO: Jamaica Tourist Board, (800) 233-4582, or http://www.jamaicatravel.com

MEXICO
RESIDENCY REQUIREMENT: 2 days
NECESSARY DOCUMENTS: Certified copies
of birth certificates previously "legalized" and
translated by the Mexican consulate with
jurisdiction over the place of birth; driver's
licenses or passports; certified proof of divorce
or death certificates of former spouse/s (if
applicable) previously "legalized" by the Mexican
consulate with jurisdiction over the place of filing;
judge's form; tourist cards; Mexican-performed
blood test results and X-rays, names, addresses,
ages, nationalities of 4 witnesses. Some cities
require Mexican witnesses.
NOTE: The marriage requirements in Mexico vary
from city to city and judge to judge.
MORE INFO: Mexico Tourism Board, (800) 446-
3942

Puerto Rico:
RESIDENCY REQUIREMENT: None
NECESSARY DOCUMENTS: ID card or Passports
or certified copies of birth certificates; Original
birth certificate from previously married brides,
proof of divorce or death certificate of former
spouse/s (if applicable);
NOTE:
MORE INFO: Health certificate from a resident
practitioner in Puerto Rico, written parental
consent if either party is under 21 years old

ST. KITTS & NEVIS
RESIDENCY REQUIREMENT: 2 working days (not
including Saturday or Sunday)

NECESSARY DOCUMENTS: Passports; original, "apostillized" birth certificates and two photo IDs; if applicable, "apostillized" proof of divorce or death certificates of former spouse/s
NOTE: If Catholic priest to perform, must have letter from home stating couple is unmarried, If Anglican, same is applicable.
MORE INFO: stkittsnevis.net

ST. MAARTEN
RESIDENCY REQUIREMENT: 10 days
NECESSARY DOCUMENTS: Passports; original, "apostillized" birth certificates and two photo IDs; if applicable, "apostillized" proof of divorce or death certificates of former spouse/s
NOTE: Requests must be made 14 days in advance. You must be at least 21 years of age to marry in St. Maarten. The French side of the island, St. Martin, has prohibitive residency requirements.
MORE INFO: Office of Civil Registry, (011) 5995-22457

EUROPE:

ENGLAND
RESIDENCY REQUIREMENT: 15 days
NECESSARY DOCUMENTS: Passports or certified copies of birth certificates; proof of divorce or death certificate of former spouse/s (if applicable)MORE INFO: Visit Britain, (800) 462-2748; British Consulate General, (212) 745-0200; or http://www.britainusa.com

SCOTLAND
RESIDENCY REQUIREMENT: None

NECESSARY DOCUMENTS: Passports or certified copies of birth certificates; proof of divorce or death certificate of former spouse/s (if applicable); certificate of no impediment
NOTE: Notice must also be sent to the registrar at least six weeks (but no longer than three months) in advance of the wedding.
MORE INFO: Visit Britain, (800) 462-2748; British Consulate General, (212) 745-0200; or http://www.britainusa.com

South Pacific:

FIJI
RESIDENCY REQUIREMENT: None
NECESSARY DOCUMENTS: Passports; birth certificates; notarized letters of paternal consent if under 21; proof of divorce or death certificate of former spouse/s (if applicable).
NOTE: Registration formalities take about 15 minutes (you both must appear) but paperwork processing takes one working day. Other requirements vary by church. MORE INFO: Fiji Visitors Bureau, (800) 932-3454, or http://www.bulafiji.com

THAILAND
RESIDENCY REQUIREMENT: None
NECESSARY DOCUMENTS: Passports; proof of divorce and/or death certificate for former spouses/s (if applicable); "Letters of Certification" from the embassy of those getting married, translated and certified by the Ministry of Foreign Affairs
MORE INFO: U.S. Embassy in Thailand at fax

(011) 66-2-205-4103 or http://www.thai-la.net

GREECE
RESIDENCY REQUIREMENT: None
NECESSARY DOCUMENTS: It is possible to use an
American marriage license - but only if it meets
certain requirements; passports; certified birth
certificates; proof of divorce or death certificate
of former spouse/s (if applicable); certificate from
U.S. Consulate in Athens, stating that there is no
impediment to the marriage; two announcements
in local Greek newspaper (one announcement for
each person)
NOTE: Greek tourism officials advise that
gathering and preparing required documents
could take a few months. All documents must
be translated into Greek by the Greek consulate
in your area. The Greek National Tourist
Organization, (212) 421-5777, will fax instructions
and supply names of companies that specialize
in arranging weddings for foreigners. Greek law
does not provide for certain interfaith marriages
such as Christians to non-Christians or Jews to
non-Jews. Proof of religion, such as baptismal
certificates, may be required.
MORE INFO: Greek National Tourist Organization,
(212) 421-5777, or the Greek Consulate, (212)
988-5500

HAWAII
RESIDENCY REQUIREMENT: None
NECESSARY DOCUMENTS: Driver's license or
passport; no proof of divorce is necessary, but
those who are divorced must be able to provide
the date, state, and county (or country) where

the divorce was finalized

NOTE: Licenses must be filed with the state health department office in Honolulu, or call the department for listings of agents in rural communities. Forms require the names of parents and their places of birth. Both parties must appear in person.

MORE INFO: Hawaii's Department of Health marriage licensing office or (808) 586-4544; or http://www.gohawaii.com

ITALY

RESIDENCY REQUIREMENT: 4 days

NECESSARY DOCUMENTS: Passports or armed forces ID cards; certified copies of birth certificates; proof of divorce or death certificate of former spouse/s (if applicable); declarations "atto notorio" sworn to by two people before an Italian consulate attesting that they know of no reason to object to the marriage under the laws of the couple's home country; declaration sworn to by both parties that there are no obstacles to the marriage under U.S. law

NOTE: Certain documents must be translated into Italian with apostille seals from the secretary of state from the state from which the documents originated. Additional requirements apply if one of the parties is an Italian citizen or resident of Italy. Requirements may vary by region and city.

MORE INFO: Italian consulate nearest you; the Italian Government Travel Office, (212) 245-5618; the local U.S. Embassy or Consulate in Italy, www.usembassy.it

The grid below shows the high and low seasons for various destination wedding locations:

Destination	Most Expensive/High	Least Expensive/Low
Caribbean	December 15-April15	July through November
Hawaii	June – August, Christmas – Easter	September, Early December
South Pacific	May-September	December-February
Mexico	Mid-December – March	April-October